MW00931873

How To Stop Drinking Without Willpower: The Unusual Way A Family Man Quit Drinking For Good

By Craig Beck

Published by Craig Beck Media 2003-2018
www.CraigBeck.com
www.StopDrinkingExpert.com

How To Stop Drinking Without Willpower
Copyright Craig Beck Media Limited

www.stopdrinkingexpert.com

Craig Beck (The Stop Drinking Expert) was a well-regarded family man with two children, a lovely home, and a successful media career; a director of several companies, and at one time the trustee of a large children's charity.

Craig was a successful and functioning professional man in spite of a 'two bottles of wine a night' drinking habit. For 20 years, he struggled with problem drinking, all the time refusing to label himself an alcoholic because he did not think he met the stereotypical image that the word portrayed.

He tried numerous ways to cut down; attempting 'dry months', banning himself from drinking spirits, only drinking at the weekend and on special occasions (and found that it is astonishing how even the smallest of occasions can suddenly become 'special').

All these 'will-power' based attempts to stop drinking failed (exactly as they were destined to do). Slowly he discovered the truth about alcohol addiction, and one by one, all the lies he had previously believed started to fall apart. For the first time, he noticed that he genuinely did not want to drink anymore. In this book, he will lead you through the same remarkable process.

The Stop Drinking Expert method is unique...

• No labels – you are not an alcoholic!
• A permanent cure. Not a lifetime struggle.
• No embarrassing Alcoholics Anonymous
• Forget about expensive rehab.
• Zero ineffective willpower required.
• No dangerous medication.
• Treats the source of the problem, not the symptoms.

- 5x more effective than traditional methods.

Over the past decade, Craig has become recognized as the world's #1 quit drinking mentor. He has helped over 50,000 people to discover their own happy sober life.

Craig also offers personal support and a series of unique tool to help you stop drinking alcohol in his online club – which has helped many thousands of people to quit and stay quit:

www.stopdrinkingexpert.com

Published Monday, March 12, 2018

Elaine Masterson
1 review

Amazing, Highly Recommended.

When I started reading this book I was only intending to cut down my drinking, but one chapter in I'd resolved to stop drinking completely (having been a drinker for 30 years or so). I'm pleased to say it's the best decision I ever made and that was almost a year and a half ago now. I cannot recommend this book highly enough. It's message is so good that it takes willpower out of the equation completely. Thank you Craig Beck!

 Useful 2

"Excellent"
☑ TRUSTPILOT

Worried about your drinking?

Not sure if you should quit drinking completely or if you should just cut back?

Reserve your free place on the daily 'Quit Drinking Without Willpower' Webinar:

https://events.genndi.com/channel/howtoquitdrinking

What's covered in this quit drinking event...

Do you really have a problem with alcohol?

How bad is your drinking compared to other people? We will talk about how you know when it is time to take action and whether you should quit completely or just cut back.

6

Why you are not an alcoholic and AA have it all wrong.

You are not broken or weak-willed. I will show you how this devious drug has tricked you over the years and how you quickly break free from the illusion.

Why is having 'just one drink' so difficult?

How many times have you promised yourself that you will have only one drink? I will show you why this simple goal is virtually impossible to achieve.

How do you relax without alcohol?

If you are drinking every night to 'relax' or deal with stress then this part of the webinar is a must see for you.

Chapter One
Sick & Tired of Feeling Sick & Tired?

"Nothing else has worked for me. AA, Rehab, Counseling, Willpower... it wasn't until I found Craig on YouTube that I realized why nothing had worked. His thoughts, ideas, and program are just simply amazing, and it takes practically no convincing on his part to make you realize how evil alcohol is and how your life is so much better without it. Just the things he says hit me so profoundly that it made it easy to just stop.

Of course, some parts of his how to stop drinking process aren't as easy, but he gets you through that as well. I have read a LOT of books and watched a lot of videos and nothing has come close to the help Craig has given me, and tons of others.

Thank you, Craig, for your fantastic work", ", Sarah Sanchez

Do you have a problem with alcohol?

Most people pick up this book with that 'do I have a problem?' question on their mind. Some are hoping this book will allow them to conclude that they are doing nothing wrong and now conveniently have some written evidence to back up and endorse the continuation of their habit. Others are aware that they are no longer in control and want help to stop drinking and to then stay quit. Stopping drinking, as we all know, is the easy bit. Staying permanently off the booze is the real problem.

So let's answer that initial burning question… Do you have a problem with alcohol?

Yes, but there is not actually anyone who drinks alcohol that doesn't have a problem. Alcohol is in itself a problem and not a solution (as many believe it to be). Therefore if this substance is in your life 'in any form', you cannot help but have a problem. As you will discover in this book, alcohol is an addictive toxin packaged into attractive bottles, marketed with billions of dollars of advertising and so deeply ingrained in popular culture that we can no longer see it for what it really is.

One thing you will quickly discover is that people get very upset when you criticize this drug, they don't even like you referring to it as a drug! Your alcohol-drinking friends would tell me to stop being so melodramatic. They will probably argue that many millions of people around the world manage to enjoy alcohol responsibly and it doesn't negatively affect their lives in the slightest. Some might go further to suggest that for some the occasional drink improves or enhances their life. However, this counter-argument to my opening gambit only holds water if you suspend the reality that alcohol is actually a poison created from the by-product of decaying vegetable waste.

This book is all about opening your eyes to what is going on behind the smoke and mirrors of alcohol. In truth, alcohol is a poison (a registered poison no less)! So with that fact in mind how can anyone argue that the habitual consumption of poison is a positive thing?

Many people find this concept tricky to take on board initially because we are conditioned to see alcohol, not as a poison but merely a harmless social pleasantry. So for the sake of argument, let's replace the poison used in this argument with a different toxin, hydrogen cyanide for example. Imagine how illogical it would be to try and defend the consumption of cyanide!

Would you say that someone who only consumes cyanide infrequently was a social user or normal user of the chemical? Yet, this is exactly what we do with alcohol. Of course, your first response to this will probably be an objection to the comparison. Many will complain that cyanide will kill you stone dead, whereas alcohol just makes you merry. It is true that neat cyanide will kill you but then so will 100% pure alcohol. Heavily diluted cyanide won't kill you, but it will make you very ill… are we really a million miles away as comparisons go?

Once you become aware that the emperor isn't actually wearing any clothes at all, and realize that alcohol is none of the things the marketing suggests it is, only then can you start to deconstruct some of the popular language surrounding its use. We talk of these 'normal' and 'social drinkers', the people who can consume alcohol at parties and social occasions but don't appear to be dependent on it to remain functional. Of course, even the most hardened alcoholic at some point was what we would describe as a 'social drinker'; before the mousetrap of alcoholism snapped closed on them, they were considered just as normal as the next guy. The poor problem drinkers looked at them and wondered why they couldn't drink for fun, just like them.

And so the cycle of addiction continues; social drinkers slowly become alcohol dependent problem drinkers, and instantly in the eyes of society they stop being 'normal' and become weak-willed, pitifully sad people who, for some reason, can't consume an addictive toxin and stay in control of it. Alcohol is many things, but it certainly is none of the glitzy life-enhancing things we are told by the advertising agencies or collectively endorsed lies that have been handed down from generation to generation.

We believe that booze makes a party go with a swing, and yet the next day we happily use words of destruction to describe what a great time we had. We stare out from blood shot eyes, with a tongue feeling like a butcher's chopping block, and gleefully report that last night we were 'trashed, slaughtered, mashed, hammered, destroyed, wasted' or a hundred other different terrible adjectives that now apparently mean something good happened.

The marketing for alcohol would have you believe that simply drinking their specific brand of attractively packaged poison will turn you into the next Brad Pitt or Elle MacPherson. In reality, we know how good a drunk actually looks to us when we are sober. Whether they are male or female, there is perhaps nothing less attractive than having someone come up to you stinking of booze, slurring a badly thought out chat up line, as a little bit of saliva drips from the corner of their mouth. Forget the advertising spiel, the only way you can get you more sex while on alcohol is to find someone who is equally as drunk as you.

Does it really make you a sex symbol if you have to use a drug to get the opposite sex to sleep with you?

The more you think about what you are doing, the more ridiculous it appears. We create lots of distractions to avoid the truth about this drug. We claim it is essential to a good party; we think it makes food taste better and we connect it to social standing. You must surely have heard that if you can afford to pay astronomical amounts of money for your alcohol that makes you a connoisseur, and a person who appreciates the finer things in life (not an alcoholic). Listen to a 'wine expert' talk about the latest vintage to come out of the

Bordeaux region, and you would think they were describing bottled sex. They talk of a seductive nose and a robust body with a hint of dark chocolate and wild berries. As you will discover in this book, it's all just the ego creating illusions of grandeur to cover up a bad habit that it would rather you keep up (because it feels nice, or rather it stops an unpleasant sensation of self-induced pain). Intelligent and wealthy people have simply found a way to put a veil of acceptability and snobbery over a common drug addiction.

Back when I was a drinker, I too got trapped into this illusion of finery and alcohol going hand in hand. I allowed myself to believe that the ritual of carefully selecting a very expensive bottle of wine. Carefully selecting it from my temperature controlled wine cellar, decanting the precious liquid into an exquisite crystal jug, before holding the glass aloft to admire the deep color and rich aroma from the wine meant that I wasn't a problem drinker; I was an expert admiring a piece of art. Some of this 'art' would cost me in the region of $500 a bottle.

Yes, we might have had to forego the annual family vacation to save money, but not surprisingly my cellar was never forced to endure such austerity measures. My wine cellar was apparently never short of cash, even in the toughest times. Such was the depth of my delusion! How strange that those expensive bottles of art were bought with the intention to 'show off' to friends with, and yet they were actually normally opened after a bad day at work, sitting alone as I tried to convince myself that I deserved the liquid gold I was consuming. Daddy was not to be disturbed my wife would tell the children as they were stopped in their tracks on route to excitedly tell me about their day at school.

I was just another druggy lying to myself in my basement. I would take a noisy slurp of the fine vintage, drawing the air over the liquid on my palette, and write detailed tasting notes in my journal. Oh yes, I was a connoisseur of the highest order, I could hold my own with even the most seasoned of wine critics.

One Friday evening, I took my wife Denise out to an expensive French restaurant as a treat (of course she was driving, she always was), and as we walked into the elegantly lit restaurant, the wine Sommelier recognized me, his face lit up with a beaming smile. Walking over to us, he warmly greeted me and shook my hand, asking how I was and how the family was doing. He no more than nodded a welcome in my wife's direction before ushering us to the best table in the house. Before we had a chance to sit he told me that he had just that week taken delivery of the 2003 Chateaux Pontet Canet, it was simply divine he assured me as he walked off to get a bottle.

Denise glanced at the wine list; this particular vintage was $350.00 a bottle. She gave me one of 'those looks' that perfectly encapsulated her feelings about the matter, words were not necessary. I knew she was thinking the kids need new school uniforms and here you are considering blowing it all on one bottle of wine. When the wine waiter returned and proudly presented the label of the bottle to me, I explained it was a little too expensive. He nodded a non-judgmental smile but shot my wife a disapproving glance. He knew I was an easy sale, but there was an irritating voice of reason present who had spoilt it. He recommended a cheaper but still expensive alternative and poured us each a glass while we enjoyed our appetizers.

When our glasses reached a slurp or two away from empty, he returned with several more wide-bodied glasses, each with an inch or so of dark-colored, full-bodied red wine pre-poured into them. He placed them all down in front of me, and to my surprise and my wife's disgust, he pulled up a chair to join us. He sat to my side with his back to Denise; reaching across the table to push the first glass towards me.

"I would value your opinion Mr. Beck, these are on the house, just tell me what you think", he said with a huge smile. If he could see the expression on the face of my wife, I doubt he would have been so cheerful!

I should have seen that this guy had hi-jacked what should have been a romantic candlelit meal. In truth I had never planned it as such; it was just another evening activity that I could do that didn't interfere with my drinking. I could just have easily taken my wife to the theatre, but then I would have only been able to drink before the show and during the interval. A restaurant with alcohol on tap was a much better option, and besides, it was too late, my ego had already kicked in; I was flattered to be considered such an expert that this experienced wine waiter would value my opinion so highly. I felt about as significant as you can get, my ego was at pleasure level ten.

I picked up the vast glass, cupped it in the palm of my hand and began the performance us wine aficionados like to give when consuming our favorite drug. I slurped loudly, rolled my tongue around, inspected the color against the candlelight and declared my verdict. "Bravo!" he cheered, almost giddy with excitement at my approval. Another glass was pushed forward, and another, and another, until a full thirty minutes had passed by. I don't know how much spectacularly expensive wine I consumed gratis that night, but my, what a splendid evening I thought it to be.

I got home elated (and drunk), crowing about the extraordinary service and attention we had received all evening. My wife frowned at me and walked up the stairs to bed. She didn't say anything about the evening until the next time I suggested we go to the same restaurant. Her memory of the previous visit seemed to be in direct contrast with my own. She talked about the rude and unprofessional waiter who had ignored her all night and hogged my attention, boring her to death by droning on and on about his wine cellar. The scene she

17

was describing shocked me, it was so far removed from what I had experienced, I even considered that she had maybe been there on a different occasion with someone else. I was much more willing to consider my wife was having an affair than that she didn't enjoy all the free booze we got that night.

Of course, her memories of the night were not clouded by vast qualities of a mind-altering drug. She was right, and I was just another problem drinker who had found a smoke screen to cover my habit that actually worked. I was drinking one or two bottles of expensive, attractively packaged poison a night, but had managed to delude myself that there was nothing wrong in that. I couldn't have a problem because I was clearly a cut above the alcoholic in the park who chugged back super-strength tins of beer. I was buying and drinking the stuff of kings, this was an indication of my social standing and refined palette, and surely not a proclamation of a drug addiction!

Bullshit! Whether your smoke screen is the same as mine or you have managed to create another entirely different one, it's still just bullshit and nothing more. The sooner you grow up and admit this, the better. It doesn't matter whether you drink cheap plonk or expensive wine, it's all the same thing. Alcohol kills just as many intelligent and wealthy people as it does poor and deprived, it doesn't care how much you spent on your habit. The doctor won't cut you open one day and declare you to have the correct type of liver failure and thank goodness you drank the posh stuff and not that horrible cheap cider.

Let me quote you what the world heath organization says about your drug of choice, and then let me ask you if at any point they refer to the type or quality of the alcohol being consumed:

The harmful use of alcohol is a global problem that compromises both individual and social development. It results in 2.5 million deaths each year. Alcohol is the world's third largest risk factor for premature mortality, disability, and loss of health; it is the leading risk factor in the Western Pacific and the Americas and the second largest in Europe. Alcohol is associated with many serious social and developmental issues, including violence, child neglect and abuse, and absenteeism in the workplace. It also causes harm far beyond the physical and psychological health of the drinker. It harms the well-being and health of people around the drinker. An intoxicated person can harm others or put them at risk of traffic accidents or violent behavior, or negatively affect co-workers, relatives, friends or strangers. Thus, the impact of the harmful use of alcohol reaches deep into society.

Stop deluding yourself that you are part of something greater, or a member of a special elite club. A bottle of wine a night makes you no better than the homeless person swigging supermarket's own label whiskey in the park. Your bottle may have a pretty label, but inside the poison remains the same.

You might assume that cigarette smoking is the world's biggest killer and you would be correct. However, that fact is only true when you apply it to the full spectrum of social demographics. Low paid manual workers and the elite with their expensive Cubans and such add a disproportionate number to that figure. Actually when you consider the middle-income earners, then alcohol becomes the true grim reaper.

One of my favorite arguments to prove I was doing nothing wrong was to state loudly and proudly 'hey at least I don't smoke'. I would say this because I felt it proved that I could be doing something much worse – of course along with all the other lies I believed, it was just alcoholic smoke and mirrors.

Alcohol is known as the silent killer because so many assume that they would be able to recognize the signs of a problem early enough to simply stop. The fact that they even consider this illogical nonsense as a safety net is evidence in itself that the mousetrap has already been primed. It's exactly the same as the mouse assuming he would have enough time to avoid the steel trap bar and its deadly spike before it got the chance to hit him.

With the problem drinker, this one assumption is the mother of all mistakes, because the organ most at risk of fatal damage from alcohol is the liver. This unique part of the body is a piece of natural engineering that way surpasses the label 'genius'. This one organ is responsible for hundreds of vital functions in the healthy human body. So important is it, that it even has the ability to repair itself and can even continue to function with up to seventy percent of its surface area damaged. Now you might think, why would anyone continue drinking if they had already done that much damage to their liver?

The problem is, the liver has very few nerve endings in it, and so you are simply unaware of the damage being caused by the alcohol. Only when the organ itself becomes so swollen from the abuse that it begins to press on other more sensitive areas of the abdomen, do addicts begin to feel something wrong and start to worry they have caused some damage.

As I am sure you can appreciate; when a human organ is so badly swollen that it is pressing on other parts of the body with enough pressure to cause pain, it must be in a pretty shocking state. Sadly, it is often only at this point that people think about going to the doctor, but often will put if off as long as possible for fear that (god forbid) the doctor insists that they stop drinking. Often by the time they reach the point where they can't sleep for the pain and can't avoid the GP any longer do they go and get the tests. Many, at this point find out that the damage is irreversible and the only option is a liver transplant.

So you get a liver transplant, and everything is fine again, right?

Wrong! There are currently 18,000 people in the United States awaiting a liver transplant. Where do you think you would rank on the waiting list next to the child who was perhaps born with a defective liver, or the woman seriously injured in an automobile wreck. Health services around the world don't look too kindly on people like you who had a perfectly good liver and opted to destroy it. Plus, they assume that you will only go on to abuse the donor organ too, and so you may never see the top of that waiting list.

So subtle is the drug that most problem drinkers are not aware of the precise moment that control was lost and they became alcohol dependent. There certainly is no point trying to work out when you changed from being a 'social' drinker of poison to an addicted drinker of poison.

The only fair assumption to make is that anyone who starts drinking alcohol socially inadvertently primes the mousetrap the moment they take their first sip. Some people will be destroyed by the mechanism and others may never feel the harm, but the only true way to ensure you don't get squashed is to never try and grab that cheese and stay well away from the trap in the first place.

Everyone who drinks alcohol is in the cycle. All those strangers, friends and colleagues you wrongly assume are somehow better than you because they apparently can take or leave a drink are still all mice sitting blissfully unaware of the danger. The steel bar may snap closed on them next week, next year, in ten years time or maybe they will sit there for a lifetime. The only constant is, as long as they continue to consume the addictive drug alcohol, they continue to play a very dangerous game of booze buckaroo™, and you have seen what happens when that mule eventually kicks!

Society insists that there is a profound difference between the people who drink a few bottles of wine a week, and a person who drinks to excess on a daily basis. The latter is described as suffering from an illness called alcoholism; they are labeled as alcoholics and forced by well-meaning support groups to identify themselves by the same derogatory nametag. They are told that they have a condition that is incurable and must for the rest of their life describe themselves as a 'recovering alcoholic'.

Perhaps this bleak and depressing ritual explains why 95% of people who turn to organizations such as Alcoholics Anonymous fail to stop drinking. This book is certainly not here to put down the efforts of this organization, or any other method, because for the 5% of people who do escape from the loop using the Big

Book theory of alcohol cessation, the rewards are truly life-changing.

The reason AA doesn't work for most people is because it requires its members to use 'will-power' to quit. This is the default weapon for human beings when they identify something in their life that is not serving them. From trying to lose weight to giving up an addictive drug, we always assume the best course of action is to force ourselves to stay away from the thing we crave. The very idea of 'will-power' is an oxymoron, there is actually no power at all in 'will-power, ' and later I will explain more about this.

Drinking alcohol is akin to juggling with fire sticks, there is a decent chance you will get burned. The difference in this comparison is you wouldn't then label the people who got injured by the flame as incurable 'fireaholics'. We would be more likely to say that they, unfortunately, got hurt, as the result of playing with a substance that used in the wrong context is dangerous. Using fire for anything other than cooking and heating is not a safe activity (exactly why we scold our children for playing with matches). Using alcohol for anything other than its chemically defined uses as a disinfectant, germicide or fuel is asking for trouble. When trouble inevitably arrives with this use of this drug, we choose to blame the person and not the substance that actually caused the damage.

You are not an alcoholic, nor are you weak willed or suffering from an addictive personality. You are none of those things, over 80% of the western world consumes alcohol, and 80% of those people are no longer in control.

If you watch the glamour adverts for the latest designer vodka in high rotation across our television screens, you may find that hard to believe. Alcohol appears to be, if not the reason for the party in the first place, the life, and soul of its success. Alcohol is potentially the most dangerous and deceptive drug on planet earth! Over dramatic? As we progress on this journey together, I will explain why this is the case.

Let me tell you here and now, you are most certainly not alone; thousands and thousands of people just like you lose control of alcohol every day. That one little drink to help them unwind at the end of a busy day, or the quick pint with friends has turned from a 'like to have' to a 'must have'. As with all drink related problems, this doesn't happen overnight, you don't wake up one morning an 'alcoholic'. These problems develop slowly over 5 to 20 years, so slowly you don't even see them coming. Such is the viciously deceptive nature of this drug that initially there are no negative symptoms to indicate the beginning of a serious problem. As a matter of fact, for most people, the beginning of a long battle with alcohol will appear to be woven with an array of positives. Early stage problem drinkers may feel lively, confident and carefree when they drink. Eventually, they become known for being 'able to handle their booze', as though this is a positive trait to be proud of. Often these people are described as party animals or the life and soul of any occasion. So while the chemical is working on your brain, your friends and colleagues are working on your ego, a powerful combination indeed.

Many people buy this book not to stop drinking, but rather with the goal of proving to themselves, or even to the caring family members or friends who have questioned their drinking. That they don't have a problem with alcohol. I can sugar coat this next section for you if you wish, I could spend several chapters building up to it, but let's cut to the chase, and you can decide whether you want to disagree before we go any further together. Let me fire some questions at you:
• Have you ever planned your day based on the availability of alcohol?

• Have you ever made rules for yourself about your drinking, e.g., I will only drink beer and no hard spirits?

• Has anyone ever questioned you about your drinking?

• Have you ever tried to stop or cut down your drinking and failed before?

A YES to any of those questions my friend, means you have a problem with alcohol. I deliberately don't call you an alcoholic because I know your automatic conditioned response is to defend yourself in the face of such an assault on your perception of who you are. Regardless of how blatant the problem and symptoms appear to be, if you label someone an alcoholic you will quickly get sold the line 'I admit I drink too much, but I am most certainly not an alcoholic'. I understand this objection because despite the fact that I consumed on average over 120 units of alcohol a week, and for a period of nearly ten years, I still refused to declare myself to be an alcoholic. To this day I point blank refuse to accept that label; I do not believe any of the thousands of people who have stopped drinking via this method are either. You are no more alcoholic than an individual who is constantly scratching his head could be said to be a 'scratchaholic'. Alcohol misuse is the symptom of a problem and not the actual problem itself.

Many people think of alcoholics as disheveled, homeless winos who have lost everything, but there are people who meet the criteria for a medical diagnosis for alcohol dependence who are highly functional in society and still have their jobs, homes, and families. This type of drinker is known as a functional alcoholic (or functional problem drinker, whatever label you want to apply). They rarely miss work and other obligations because of their drinking, although it does happen occasionally. They usually excel at their jobs and careers. Typically, they are knowledgeable and witty individuals who are successful in many areas of their lives. To all but those who are closest to them, they give the outward appearance of being perfectly unremarkable.

I know who these people are because I used to be one. I kept my drinking hidden through some of the most successful periods of my career in broadcasting. If you also have a problem with this drug that is currently kept hidden away from your colleagues and family, in this book, I will show you how to take control of the situation without anyone needing to know you ever had a problem in the first place.

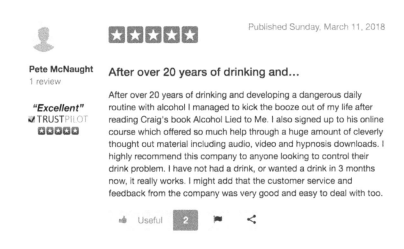

Published Sunday, March 11, 2018

Pete McNaught
1 review

"Excellent"
☑ TRUSTPILOT
★★★★★

After over 20 years of drinking and…

After over 20 years of drinking and developing a dangerous daily routine with alcohol I managed to kick the booze out of my life after reading Craig's book Alcohol Lied to Me. I also signed up to his online course which offered so much help through a huge amount of cleverly thought out material including audio, video and hypnosis downloads. I highly recommend this company to anyone looking to control their drink problem. I have not had a drink, or wanted a drink in 3 months now, it really works. I might add that the customer service and feedback from the company was very good and easy to deal with too.

👍 Useful 2 🚩 ＜

Chapter Two
Hey! I Can Stop Anytime I Want

"This program can work for ANYONE! I have tried many things, mostly on my own for over ten years. If you are ready, the tools that Craig provides are all you need.

The company's service is prompt, knowledgeable, personable and will go above and beyond if you need extra help.

Commit to it; Craig can educate, dispel doubts, banish excuses and give strength to ANYONE. Type A, Intellectual, Educated, or Not, Atheist or Faithful, Hopeful or Hopeless. You have landed in the right place; this can be your answer if you follow the program.

How do I know?

Happily sober, going on five weeks, does that not sound like much time to you? Well, considering that I haven't been able to string more than a couple of sober weeks together in 17 Years, I'll take it! Confident in the knowledge that I will never drink poison again", Karen Lanese

Denial is a problem and not just a river in Egypt!
One of the main reasons that alcoholics seek help for
their drinking problems is the eventual negative
consequence of their alcohol consumption. When the
pain or embarrassment gets bad enough, they can no
longer deny that their drinking needs to be addressed.
For the functional alcoholic, the denial runs deep,
because they have yet to encounter outward negative
consequences to their habit.

They go to work every day. They haven't suffered
financially. Most have never been arrested or on the
wrong side of the law. From their point of view, they
simply can't have a problem because they don't fit their
definition of what a person with a drinking problem
should look like! Don't blame television, Hollywood or
it's actors, they are compelled to keep portraying
alcoholics as the staggering, slurring down and outs
that we are familiar with. If a director instructed his
leading man to play an alcoholic character as a
functional alcoholic, how would we even know he had
any sort of addiction problem?

The functional problem drinker often consumes just as
much alcohol as any fully blown alcoholic; they just
don't exhibit the outward symptoms of dependence.
This is because they have developed a tolerance for
alcohol to the point that it takes so much more for them
to feel the effects. Consequently, they must drink
increasingly larger amounts to get the high they crave.

This slow build-up of alcohol tolerance means the functional alcoholic is drinking at dangerous levels, which can result in alcohol-related organ damage, cognitive impairment and alcohol dependence. Chronic heavy drinkers can display a functional tolerance to the point that they show few obvious signs of intoxication, even at high blood alcohol concentrations, which in others would be incapacitating.

In the mid 90's, Steve McFadden, a popular British soap opera actor, was arrested and charged with driving under the influence of alcohol. He had consumed nine double vodkas before getting behind the wheel of his car. While to most people this would be enough to knock them out for the night, he decided to fight the prosecution because he claimed to have had an unusually high tolerance to alcohol. The courts witnessed the bizarre scene of a man consuming such a vast amount of drink and still appearing to be completely sober. The judge obviously bought the argument as the actor was banned for just 18 months, a very light sentence for such a large blood alcohol reading.

You need to change what alcoholic means to you; it doesn't mean you must accept being a social outcast or that the condition is permanent. Alcoholism isn't a figment of your imagination, and I will keep confirming for you that you are not weak-willed or in any way a failure because of this problem. A statement which frequently predicts the response, 'how come I can't just open a bottle of wine and have one glass with my meal?' or 'why can't I ever just have one, like my friends appear to be able to do?'

If alcoholics were weak-willed individuals, wouldn't that flaw in their personality apply to all areas of their life? If there is really such a thing as an addictive personality, then logic would dictate that the condition would apply to all areas and all alcoholics would also be obese, gambling addicted, heroin injecting, glue sniffers. You are alcoholic because of a long-term chemical imbalance exacerbated by your body's tendency to process alcohol differently from those annoying people who can just enjoy a glass of red wine with their steak and think nothing of putting the bottle away for another day.

Alcoholism is often stated to be a disease just like cancer. This is not true; a disease implies there is nothing you can do about it and that you may have contracted it without any conscious input on your part. This creates the innocent victim mentality that drinkers then use as a perfectly valid excuse for them to continue drinking to excess. Once labeled as such, they begin a 'pity party' that can last a lifetime. They declare how terrible it is to suffer from such a debilitating condition. Shrugging their shoulders, cursing their bad luck as they wash away their perceived problems with a stiff drink.

You have lost a fight that you never had any chance of winning. It is not your fault, but it absolutely is your responsibility.

Problem drinking is not a disease it is a negative behavioral loop that appears to be so complicated that it may feel as though it is unbreakable. Many people state that they drink to make their problems go away, but at the same time they are aware of all the extra problems their drinking is creating. All your beliefs about why you drink are likely to be a Catch 22 situation.

For example, you are worried about money and don't want to spend the evening thinking about all those bills and so out comes the booze. The alcohol (which is a mild anesthetic) merely time shifts your problems forward another 24 hours and then adds an additional problem of alcohol withdrawal into the mix. Remember, you started drinking to forget the bills but the booze habit is costing you thousands of dollars each year, and if you didn't spend so much feeding your alcohol addiction you would probably be able to pay all the bills you are worrying about in the first place.

The average person who stops drinking as a result of reading this book or joining my online club goes on to save over $4000 per year. While money isn't strictly speaking a good enough reason to stop on its own, it is a very pleasant by-product of quitting. If you were offered a no strings pay rise of that size, wouldn't you gladly accept it?

So if saving money is only the byproduct of the process you might be wondering what the primary reason is. We will come to that in due course, and at this point in How To Stop Drinking Without Willpower, I would like to offer you a word of warning; It's important to read this book in the order it is written and not be tempted to skip ahead to find the magic bullet cure. You will find no such thing; it is the slow deconstruction of the lies alcohol has repeatedly told you over the years, and a growing understanding of why booze affects you the way it does that allows you to see it for what it is. More importantly, to stop believing that alcohol is somehow benefiting you.

There are no real benefits to booze, only illusions of positives. Everyone who consumes alcohol has inadvertently placed himself or herself in the mousetrap; some are moments away from disaster, others are a lifetime away. Slowly the mechanism is loaded and primed, over time you become more and more at risk of letting alcohol seize control of your life. You are effectively playing a virtual version of Russian roulette, but with booze as the bullet in your loaded gun. Every time you drink you pull the trigger, and one day the chamber will not be empty. There is only one way to play this game safely, and that is to remove the bullet - or to put it another way - don't drink.

This killer product escapes virtually all our current regulations and safeguards because it has been around long enough to set its own precedent. The fact that 'everyone drinks' and our parents, grandparents, and generations as far back as we can recall also drank alcohol, makes us incorrectly believe we are protected by the assumed 'safety in numbers' principle. Actually, that is not true, no drinker really believes that he or she is protected because of the social proof of the drug, they are just pleased to have another weapon in their arsenal to justify their behaviour around a substance that we all inherently know is dangerous and unhealthy.

There is no safety in numbers with alcohol, just because everyone you know drinks does not make it a safe product, reduce your chances of getting addicted or suffering harm in some way. Whether one person plays Russian roulette or a billion people play, the odds remain the same for each person holding the gun. Every pull of the trigger is a separate unique incident and is completely independent of and uninfluenced by all the other triggers being pulled at that time. Just because the people who surround you all appear to be 'in control' of their drinking does not give you license to assume you will be affected by alcohol in a similar way.

Many people pick up this book still hanging onto the hope that they will be able to reduce their drinking down to a sensible amount. I would love to tell you that glorious compromise is possible; perhaps I would sell more books if I pretended that it is. However, integrity is important to me, and I can't tell you anything but the hard facts and truth about this drug.

Reducing the amount of poison you are consuming is as helpful to you as closing an open porthole on the Titanic. If I were to advise you to cut down, there would be an implication that drinking perhaps provides some benefits if consumed in small amounts. It doesn't, the most common objection to this statement comes from the 'red wine is good for your heart' brigade. Credit, where it is due this, is correct to a certain degree; there are indeed a lot of healthy antioxidants in a glass of red wine. But no more so than you would find in a glass of non-alcoholic grape juice, or a hand full of pomegranate seeds. If it's your heart you are concerned about, find an alternative to wine. But if you really are using that argument to continue drinking, I suspect it really has nothing to do with your health.

If wine is so good for your heart, why don't doctors break out the Merlot when a patient is rushed to hospital suffering from a heart attack?

When most people realize drinking has changed from a 'nice to have' into a 'must have' they try to cut down. If you had a reckless and thrill seeking friend who you discovered was in the habit of loading a single bullet into a revolver and playing Russian Roulette for kicks a few times a week would you really advise him to cut down and only do it at the weekend or to stop completely? In 'How To Stop Drinking Without Willpower' I am going to demonstrate in undeniable detail to you as the intelligent and informed human being I know you are, exactly why alcohol is something that you do not need, does not serve you, has absolutely no benefits to it and creates nothing but negatives in your life. Once you understand that everything you currently believe is just smoke and mirrors generated by a myriad of social and psychological sources, I won't need to help you stop drinking; you simply won't want to.

We start this journey together by discovering exactly why people drink alcohol to excess. Some will claim booze has uplifting qualities (this is simply not true as it is actually a mind anesthetic). While others will say they need it to chill out and relax, and you will discover later why this is equally as illogical. At this moment all you need to know is that there is only one reason why people get hooked on alcohol… it's an addictive drug that causes a chemical imbalance in the brain.

There are no other reasons; you are not a victim of a disease or prone to an addictive personality. There is no such thing as an addictive personality; it's just a convenient way of shifting the blame away from us to something external and apparently outside our control.

If somebody who juggles knives got accidentally stabbed by one of them, would you say it was not his fault because he has a personality that is susceptible to knife injuries? Or would you assume it was bound to happen one day?

If you take an addictive substance you will get addicted; it is an automatic and logical conclusion to your actions (it was bound to happen one day). It has nothing to do with a perceived fault in your genetic makeup. Surely if such a broad condition as an addictive personality really existed then you would be addicted to everything? You would consume mountains of mashed potato, vats of honey, kilos of sugar and so on, apportioning all blame to your damn addictive personality disorder.

The closest excuse you have to your drinking not being your fault is a possible genetic blip in your DNA that makes you predisposed to be highly likely to develop a problem with alcohol. Breakthroughs in a field of medical science called epigenetic inheritance have revealed some startling findings.

Meeri Kim, writing for the Washington Post says:

A newborn mouse pup, seemingly innocent to the workings of the world, may actually harbor generations' worth of information passed down by its ancestors.

In the experiment, researchers taught male mice to fear the smell of cherry blossoms by associating the scent with mild foot shocks. Two weeks later, they bred with females. The resulting pups were raised to adulthood having never been exposed to the smell.

When the critters caught a whiff of it for the first time, they suddenly became anxious and fearful. They were even born with more cherry-blossom-detecting neurons in their noses and more brain space devoted to cherry-blossom-smelling.

The memory transmission extended out another generation when these male mice bred, and similar results were found.

Neuroscientists at Emory University found that genetic markers, thought to be wiped clean before birth, were used to transmit a single traumatic experience across generations, leaving behind traces in the behavior and anatomy of future pups.

The study, published online Sunday in the journal Nature Neuroscience, adds to a growing pile of evidence suggesting that characteristics outside of the strict genetic code may also be acquired from our parents through epigenetic inheritance. Epigenetics studies how molecules act as DNA markers that influence how the genome is read. We pick up these epigenetic markers during our lives and in various locations on our body as we develop and interact with our environment.

Through a process dubbed "reprogramming," these epigenetic markers were thought to be erased in the earliest stages of development in mammals. But recent research — this study included — has shown that some of these markers may survive to the next generation.

In the past decade, the once-controversial field of epigenetics has blossomed. But proving epigenetic inheritance can be a daunting, needle-in-a-haystack undertaking. Researchers need to measure changes in offspring behavior and neuroanatomy, as well as tease out epigenetic markers within the father's sperm.

The DNA itself doesn't change, but how the sequence is read can vary wildly depending on which parts are accessible. Even though all the cells in our bodies share the same DNA, these markers can silence all the irrelevant genes so that a skin cell can be a skin cell, and not a brain cell or a liver cell.

Does this mean we as humans have also inherited generations of fears and experiences? Quite possibly, say scientists. Studies on humans suggest that children and grandchildren may have felt the epigenetic impact of such traumatic events such as famine, the Holocaust and the Sept. 11, 2001, terrorist attacks.

We are still scratching the surface of this new and interesting research but what this helps to explain is why children of alcoholics are much more likely to also develop a problem. Whether it is the genetic inheritance or the social conditioning is a point that will be debated for years. What this doesn't mean is you can carry on drinking while pointing an accusing finger at your parents.

If you discovered that skin cancer runs in your family would you sit in the midday sun every day and then blame your mom and dad when the bad news arrived one day?

The main reason your drinking has become a problem is down to a deficiency of important chemicals in your brain. Inside your frontal lobes, there are millions of transmitters and receivers. These control every aspect of your life and determine how you feel about literally everything you experience on a day-to-day basis. When the sun goes down at the end of the day, the drop in available light causes your brain to stop producing adrenaline and start manufacturing a neuro-chemical called melatonin, this clever chemical calms your mind and allows sleep to occur. If you take a substance that interferes with this natural process, such as caffeine, then you will find it very difficult to get to sleep because of the chemical imbalance.

Staying with the sleep example for a moment, there are a few other reasons why the chemicals may not be present in the quantity that you need for a healthy regular sleep pattern. The brain makes melatonin from another chemical called serotonin. This is what makes us feel good about ourselves; it's a happy drug naturally created by our body to manifest feelings of contentment and joy. Serotonin can only be made from an amino acid called Tryptophan. If your diet is poor or specifically lacking in foods that are a source of Tryptophan, then you will have a serotonin deficiency. As a direct result of that, you will also have a melatonin deficiency. You would experience the outcome of this condition by complaining of 'having trouble sleeping' in the short term. If this imbalance stays in place for enough time, you would then begin to label yourself as 'an insomniac'.

The other way you can have a chemical imbalance (again staying with the sleep analogy) is by being genetically predisposed to it. If you are born with Tryptophan transmitters and receivers that do not work as well as they should then you will need to consume significantly more of the amino acid in your diet than a 'normal' person to get the same result.

Incorrect brain chemistry makes you miserable!

Alcohol is a toxin that interferes with brain chemistry; unbalanced brain chemistry makes you unhappy, unsettled, stressed, and tired. All negative emotions that you believe can be fixed with a glass of the good stuff. This is a negative behavior loop like picking at a scab because it hurts. The more you pick at it the worst it gets, and yet you just can't leave it alone. You are

43

stressed because alcohol has created a chemical imbalance in your brain, so you have a drink to unwind. The alcohol goes on to create more chemical imbalances to ensure you also feel uncomfortable again the next day, ensuring the consumption of the drug continues.

If you owned a multimillion-dollar racehorse, is it fair to say that you would treat it with respect, stable it in the very best yard and feed it only the best premium food you could buy? Is it also equally reasonable to assume if you owned this valuable racehorse you probably wouldn't put poison in its food? You own a body that is quite frankly awe-inspiring in its beauty, complexity, and power, and yet you deliberately consume poison and claim you do it in the name of being social.

Thankfully, as a result of millions of years of evolution your body is pretty smart, it can sense when there is a dangerous foreign substance in the blood stream. When you ingest any toxin, your body will start a series of automatic processes to eliminate it from your system (as many a late night cab driver has discovered). First, the liver converts the alcohol into another chemical called acetaldehyde, which is less dangerous to the vital organs. Alcohol-dependent people have slowly trained and conditioned their liver to become far too efficient at processing alcohol. No sooner has the drink flowed into their liver than it is processed into acetaldehyde. This means we problem drinkers always have vast quantities of this chemical in our blood.

This causes two major problems; firstly it acts as an opiate, which as you know is highly addictive (we effectively have to deal with a continuous drug overdose). The double whammy is at such a high level these powerful chemicals have a secondary action of ripping through brain cells like napalm. It interferes with the thousands of receptors, prevents your body from absorbing minerals and vitamins and interferes with brain chemicals to such an extent that it takes months for the body to repair the damage (if you would just give it a chance).

When alcohol hits your brain, it triggers an artificial release of powerful chemicals that create a high. Every time you use alcohol to simulate this response; the receiver in your brain responsible for detecting the chemicals gets damaged a little bit more. Over time this is why you need more and more booze to create the same effect you used to get from one drink. This tolerance to alcohol is often seen as something to be proud of, especially in men. Being able to knock back ten pints of strong lager and not fall over has apparently become a clear sign of a real man. Remove the testosterone, and in reality, a tolerance is the first clear sign that alcohol has already caused significant damage.

Because of this severe chemical imbalance, you are pre-disposed to having a problem with alcohol, using will-power to try and stop is always going to be like pushing oil up a hill. Fighting brain chemicals with 'will-power' is pointless; if you have ever had a general anesthetic, you will know that when they inject you with the chemical they assess its effectiveness by challenging you to count to ten. You confidently begin the count, but somewhere around four or five, the lights go out, even if you wanted to fight the drug you would lose. There is no power in 'will-power'!

This rule applies as much to naturally generated chemicals as it does to artificial ones. If your brain is full of adrenaline you can't go to sleep. It is impossible no matter how much 'will-power' you use. A specific chemical in your brain creates all strong emotions from grief to love. Estrogen makes women want to mother and care for the young; testosterone makes men want to fight and have sex with things. Dopamine creates a feeling of contentment and so on. If you injected someone with adrenaline just before going into a cinema, it would be unreasonable of you to call him weak willed because he wouldn't sit still and watch the movie with you.

'Will-power' is completely ineffective against brain chemicals and so to stop drinking for good you have to alter the way you think about booze, you have to not drink because you genuinely don't want to, and not because you are being hard on yourself. You must ensure that you never have to use 'will-power' again. To get to this point you need to be aware that alcohol slowly turns us all into liars, we are programmed from a very young age to see alcohol as a faultless, natural, mood enhancing, confidence inducing, 'good times for all' product. And not the foul tasting, health-destroying slow poison that it really is.

Before we go any further, I need to tell you that I am not a doctor. Neither am I a self-righteous saint who has never put a foot wrong on the path of life. I am not here to judge you or heap a load of shame upon you. I am here with you now because, in essence, I am the same as you. I too, let alcohol control my life for over 17 years. The only difference between you and me now, is I am sitting outside the mousetrap looking at you sitting on it, like a greedy mouse that thinks he has discovered something amazing. Because I have been in the trap and experienced it, I know how you feel about giving up the drink. I know how many hundreds of times you have woken up ashamed of yourself, making veiled promises never to drink again. I know that you desperately want to give up this poison, but I am also deeply aware that at the same time the thought of spending the rest of your life without drink appears at first thought to be a life not worth living. The fact that you are reading this book means at some level you still believe that alcohol is a benefit to you. If you didn't believe that, then you simply wouldn't drink and you wouldn't need me.

For most alcohol dependent people, a life without a drink appears empty and pointless. You may even be tempted to throw such arguments as:

- 'How can you go to a party and not drink?
- Am I destined to be the boring, party pooper for the rest of my life?'
- 'How can I go on holiday without drinking?'
- 'What am I going to do to relax/steady my nerves/get to sleep'... you can insert your own lie here if you want – but that's really all it is – a lie!

While you can't physically see any of the particles that make up the air that we breathe, you know that it is a mix of different gases, with oxygen being the most vital. You can't point to oxygen and prove it to me, but if I approached you today and told you that there is no oxygen in air, you wouldn't give any credence to my claim. Unless you are a physicist, this probably isn't because of your irrefutable scientific knowledge or your ability to prove the existence of oxygen at the drop of a hat. It is purely because people you respect and trust have taught you this. You have been programmed to believe this from a very early age. The belief that we breathe oxygen is so engrained into the collective wisdom of society that it has become an undeniable fact.

Similarly, for thousands of years, it was a statement of fact that the earth was flat. Repetition is the mother of learning, and so beliefs that have been repeated and observed many times over and by many different people become hard-wired facts in our collective intellect.

Alcohol and celebration are natural bed fellows, right? All our perception of booze comes from society's collective opinion of it. Just as we were wrong about the earth being flat, we are collectively incorrect about what alcohol gives us. Some drinkers are so well programmed that at the mere suggestion from me that alcohol is not the nectar of the gods but rather a foul tasting, life-destroying drug, they will instantly and aggressively disagree. If you find yourself saying 'well that's wrong for a start, I genuinely do like the taste of alcohol', I can promise you here, and now you are at the point where your lies are so profound and so deeply ingrained in your subconscious that you can't even tell they are lies anymore.

With that depressing assessment established I want to give you two big reasons to be excited about where you are. Firstly, you not only bought the book but you opened it and started reading. This might sound like no big deal but let me tell you that over half the people who pick up a book to help address their drinking problem never even open it! Secondly, I am going to show you how to beat this drug in a completely easy and pain-free way. Stay with me for the rest of this book and I will prove to you not only that alcohol is vile tasting, but also that deep down inside you instinctively know this already.

Once you start to see alcohol for what it really is then stopping becomes the byproduct of your new knowledge… you don't have to do anything – it just happens of its own accord.

Ready to deal with this? Get started right now at www.StopDrinkingExpert.com

Chapter Three
The Bubble Of Unreality Around Alcohol

"Craig's knowledge so inspires me as it relates to my problem as no one else has before.

I purchased the monthly subscription after seeing the vast free help videos he has posted on YouTube. Once inside the members' area was listening to some hypnosis and being explained what is going on in such a relatable mythological way I emailed Craig who responded himself, refunded my monthly payment so I could buy the lifetime membership.

This is going to work!

No one I have ever spoken to has the knowledge, dedication, and care that this expert has. Why not go to the best the very best, what is a few hundred pounds when you will save thousands! You deserve the best kill this problem once and for all", Phil Williams

So, more than 80% of the adult population of the western world drink alcohol, more than 80% of those have a problem, and 80% of them will never admit it. The first thing you should be proud of is that you have taken a step that most people will never have the courage to take; you have admitted that you are worried. Not only that, you have paid your hard earned money and put your trust in my system to help you regain control of your drinking. I can't express this strongly enough; this small act puts you in the top 20% of people. Admitting you have a problem effectively means you are already 50% of the way down the road to full recovery.

STOP: Before you break open the champagne (or whatever your chosen brand of attractively packaged poison is), let me give you a word of warning: Despite what you have been told in the past, 'knowledge is not power,' but rather 'knowledge is only potential power!' If you do nothing with it, it's useless data. The shocking fact is that 20% of the people who buy a self-help book, DVD or course such as this one will never listen to a word, put the DVD in the player or even open the book to the first page. It's as though the act of buying the book was good enough 'for now.' It's a similar act of procrastination of all those people who proudly announce 'the diet starts Monday!' Surely, if they were committed to losing the weight, they would start the diet immediately, without delay! The diet always starts Monday because it's a free license to eat like a pig all weekend while lying to yourself that you have all the right intentions in the world to repair the damage on Monday.

By the way… the reason diets don't work for 95% of people who use them is; Diets also rely on 'will-power' and so they make you unhappy and fat, which is precisely why they have hidden a secret warning in the first three letters of the word diet.

Now you have started on this monumental journey, do not stop. Neither should you skip forward to try and find the secret or quick fix to your problem. You did not go to bed one night in control of alcohol and wake up the next morning an 'alcoholic.' This drug has taken years, sometimes even decades to alter physical pathways in your brain, there is no quick fix – but that doesn't mean it has to be painful, or that you need to suffer. The adage of 'No Pain – No Gain' does not apply here and trying to fight your way out of this situation is actually why you have failed to cut down in the past. It's going to take some effort on your behalf, and you may mess up every now and again, but you know what... it's not a big deal. You are not a robot, and as long as you keep working with me for the next 21 days, you are going to come out of this process stronger, cleaner and happier than you have been in a long, long time.

Unless of course you are STILL asking the question 'do I have a problem with drinking?' That is the question I get asked more than any other, if I had a penny for every email I have had from people describing their habits and then asking 'do you think I have a problem?' I would be well on my way to a very happy retirement.

Let me answer that question for you now by first translating the question into what I believe you are REALLY asking: 'I like drinking, but I am worried I can't stop, can you tell me I don't have a problem and make the worry go away so I can carry on?'

You have an unnatural relationship with alcohol, and that is why you are here. Regular 'social' poison drinkers don't ever think about their drinking habits, never mind search the Internet for help and advice, or go as far as to purchase a book like this. If you have to question your behavior around alcohol, it's the clearest sign you can get that alcohol has become a fixation. Try not to beat yourself up about this because, in reality, it's not possible for anyone to have a natural relationship with alcohol because it is a toxin packaged in pretty bottles. The belief that anyone can be a 'normal/social' drinker of a poison is a myth, how can it be possible to be a typical user of an addictive drug?

If a friend confided in you that he was a glue sniffer, but has kept his solvent abuse strictly limited to weekends, would you declare him a social glue sniffer? Replace glue with heroin… would your friend be a 'normal' heroin user? You may think I am going to extremes to prove a point here, but there are only two differences between alcohol and heroin, and the first is social acceptability. Drinking is socially acceptable, and heroin is not. From birth, we are exposed to booze being portrayed in a positive light, a substance that we are happy to ignore the logic of, and assume that it has some sort of smart technology behind it.

Somehow we believe alcohol can make us more aware of positive emotions and feelings, and claim it can also dampen down negative emotions and help us forget our problems. Only a substance that could change its chemical make-up could achieve this. There is nothing intelligent about alcohol, remember, it is the waste product of decaying vegetable matter, not a lab designed smart drug.

The second difference between alcohol and other class A street drugs is all about timescale. It is effortless to become addicted to heroin in a short space of time because the kick (withdrawal) is condensed into a smaller time instead of the slow build-up of discomfort that you get from alcohol withdrawal. Heroin users get massive and unbearable amounts of pain in a relatively short space of time. That is where the differences end, they both can and will try to kill you. They will both do significant permanent damage to your health, relationships, finances, and state of mind, and they will both twist your perception dramatically enough to make you believe that while they are doing all this negative stuff, they are also in some way a benefit to you at the same time.

I believe that alcohol is infinitely more deceptive than heroin because of the long and drawn out way it drags the user into a trap. Alcohol dependency can take decades to reach its peak addiction. It creeps up on you so slowly that for the longest time you have no idea your drinking has become unusual. You are encouraged to look the other way and ignore the slight of hand happening in your peripheral vision by society's love affair with this drug.

This is illogical, and at your core (subconscious) you understand this. The single most influential human need is that of self-preservation, you have no control over this. Your core program is to stay alive at all costs; it's hard-wired into every cell in your body. And every one of those cells knows that alcohol is hazardous to you. The body continually tries to warn you, but you have learned to see those warning signs as positives rather than negatives.

• We may go red in the face or start to sweat, and we lie to ourselves and see it as a sign of merriment.

• We lose our inhibitions (which are there to protect us), and we lie to ourselves that the booze has boosted our confidence and self-esteem.

• We drink so much that the brain loses control of our ability to talk, our speech becomes slurred, and yet we still don't see it as a warning that something is wrong.

• Our brains are misfiring so frequently and unpredictable that we can't walk straight, and yet we joke about it.

• Eventually, we get to the point where our body says enough is enough, it pushes the emergency button, which says I must get this poison out of the system, and it forces you to throw up. Do we listen at this point? No. We lie to ourselves that it's the sign of a good night.

• Maybe the hangover should be a sign of the damage we did, but no. We have been told over and over again since we were small that a hangover is natural. It's just what happens when you drink. Think about it if you got the same feelings the day after you ate a piece of toast, would you even consider eating toast again?

Perhaps you are here reading these words under duress; maybe a concerned family member, friend or employer bought this book for you. I can't tell you how many concerned partners I've met who are in relationships with people who resolutely insist they don't have a problem with drink. I am yet to meet a single one of these individuals that prove their partner wrong.

Part of 'How To Stop Drinking Without Willpower' is all about helping you understand how you got to where you are today, and why we are all tricked and deceived by alcohol. How this poison is packaged up into attractive looking bottles and marketed around the world with multibillion-dollar advertising campaigns. Booze is the ultimate wolf in sheep's clothing, known to liver consultants and medical professionals around the world (who diligently mop up our mess) as the silent killer. Often before you even know there is a problem, the damage is done.

Chapter Four
"Don't You Dare Call It A Drug"

"Craig is right on, and I am very grateful for his work! I have tried AA and rehab, which if anything has made the problem worse for me and contributed to a sense of shame, defectiveness, and powerlessness.

The answer indeed is changing one's perspective and view of alcohol and just not wanting it anymore. Thank you, Craig", Tresa Brazier

The great relay race of drinking nearly always starts with your parents, and indeed their parents before them, and so on. When you are born into this world, you enter as a completely helpless, weak and fragile individual driven by the need for love. Strange looking giants surround you, and over a space of time, you notice that two of these giants appear to have taken an interest in you. They feed you, care for you and love you (despite your crying and constant demands on their time).

For many years, these two people are given the accreditation of being Gods in your eyes. It is utterly inconceivable that they could ever be wrong or would ever lie or mislead you. Their words and actions are your gospel, and before the age of 5, you blindly accept information from this source without question. Everything you learn and witness at this tender age is stored permanently in your subconscious as a pure fact. In short, what you teach, show and expose your children to before the age of 5 will have a significant impact on how they turn out as adults.

Your experience with alcohol started from the moment you entered the world; it's more than likely the giants around you even used this poison to celebrate your arrival into the world. As you watched the giants popping corks out of attractive looking bottles, great smiles grew across their faces, and laughter filled the room; what a fantastic liquid this must be.

How strange that such a beautiful and unique gift is given to two happy people and they choose to herald the joyous arrival with a nice glass of a foul-tasting depressant that removes our ability to consciously experience the beautiful things going on around us.

Alcohol is a tradition that has been passed down the family line from generation to generation (like a defective gene or biological bad penny). You only need to change the drug to see the truth behind the lies. If a bunch of friends came around to your house to meet your new baby and they all insisted on taking cocaine to wet the baby's head, I am sure you would have something to say.

I can make this point even more transparent if you take a drug that has only recently become unacceptable. It's not so long back that a fine cigar was mandatory for the menfolk to welcome in a new addition to the family. These days smoking over a newborn child would be seen as the height of irresponsibility.

The story of the humble cigarette is interesting to make a comparison with. Many of my heavy drinking friends would never dream of smoking, and they believe it to be an anti-social habit and exceptionally bad for you. Across Europe, these days every packet of cigarette comes emblazoned with horrific images of diseased lungs and cancer infested bodies of smokers. But you really don't have to go too far back in time, and this collective disgust for smoking was indeed not the norm. I grew up in England in the seventies, a time when smoking was commonplace. Restaurants, theatres and in fact all public places were permanently shrouded in a thick fog of cigarette smoke. Candy stores even sold fake sugar based cigarettes and cigars so children could pretend to smoke, just like their older family members. Can you imagine the public outrage today if a confectionary company tried to promote their 'training cigarettes' for children?

At the time this was normal and unquestioned by even the most well-intentioned and intelligent of people. Go back a little further, and it seems incredible that doctors once suggested smoking as a cure for various ailments. For a long time cigarettes were even marketed as a health-enhancing product. It took decades for that opinion to change and even now the job is still less than only half done.

Still, the overriding opinion of western society is that smoking is much worse for you than drinking alcohol. However, according to the World Health Organization's chart of what is most likely to kill us; tobacco use ranks sixth. What surprises most people is alcohol on that very same chart comes in at third, wiping out over 2,500,000 people every year. Not bad going for a harmless social pleasantry!

Let's return to the thought of smoking over a newborn baby in this day and age. I know there will be some objections that it is not a fair comparison. You may object and claim that smoking over a newborn is only dangerous because of the passive smoke you are enforcing the baby to inhale. As it is not possible to passively drink, it cannot be reasonably compared to drinking. This is correct in physical terms but remember, everything you see at this impressionable age is received as a pure fact. From the child's point of view, why would one of the loving giants do something that is dangerous or wrong? Essentially, if their God drinks and it makes them happy, it must be something beautiful. Over the space of a few years, the child will witness many thousands of occasions where pleasure is linked to alcohol. Birthday parties, Christmas, Mothers Day, Valentines Day and even family BBQ's. Repetition is the mother of all learning.

It's the same reason why it's unthinkable to consider throwing a party without having alcoholic drinks. You do it because it's always been done, but if your parents had not passed the poison chalice onto you, and you don't pass it onto your children, the tradition becomes diluted and eventually ineffectual. We don't have to conduct an extravagant experiment over several generations to prove this point. You only need to look at other cultures; Hinduism has many festivals and celebrations that are full of merriment, singing and dancing without a single drop of alcohol passing anyone's lips.

Alcohol does not make a party – people do! But just try throwing a party in your part of the world without any alcohol and half your guests will leave and go to the nearest pub. It's not that drinking creates fun, it's more that people who are out of control of their drinking are miserable without alcohol and can't think about anything else when they are without it. This isn't the fault of your party; it's the fault of a society that teaches every one of us how to get addicted to a powerful and deceptive drug and then compounds the problem by making us believe that it's normal.

Most people who drink wine everyday claim they honestly like the taste of it. This is nonsense; alcohol tastes so bad that the drinks manufacturers essentially have to find increasingly potent ways to cover it up. The body is an amazing and sophisticated piece of natural engineering. Despite what lies you have taught yourself on a superficial level, you still cannot break the rules your body has created over millions of years of evolution. Right at the top of our hierarchy of needs is the need to protect life, to stay alive at all costs. This is hardwired into every cell, every molecule and every tiny atom of your being. You can't decide to stop your heart beating or never to breathe again. You can't because it breaks the ultimate built-in rule; that of ensuring self-preservation at all costs.

The reason pure alcohol tastes bad is the same reason rotting meat or moldy, fungus-infested bread tastes bad. Your body is warning you that you are consuming something that is putting you at risk. Think about it, in a hospital operating theatre, the room and the entire medical team that works in it must be 100% free of germs, bacteria, and viral contaminants. So what do they scrub their hands with; not soap but alcohol. Because instantly on contact with any living organisms, it kills them! It pulls every bit of moisture out of their cells and causes them to implode in on themselves. At a microcellular level, alcohol is akin to thermonuclear war; nothing survives. Do you honestly believe you have some fantastic internal system to get around this fact? Somehow, when you consume this dangerous disinfectant, it doesn't do the same level of damage because you have hidden it in a bit of cranberry juice.

Alcohol tastes horrible, you already know this but have forgotten, or as is more accurate, you have conditioned yourself to believe the opposite. As a hypnotherapist, I can tell you that this is entirely possible and can be easily replicated in a relatively short space of time to prove the point. In hypnosis, the conscious (thinking and judging) mind is bypassed, which means I can speak directly to the subconscious and implant beliefs without interference from the ego. Obviously, in therapy (and what you will find on the hypnosis tracks that accompany this book – available in the member's area) all suggestions are positive and delivered for your benefit. However, it is entirely possible for me to condition you to enjoy something deeply unpleasant, such as a hard punch on the arm! If while under hypnosis I hit you hard but told you it felt amazing and repeated that process many times and over several sessions, you would eventually begin to crave the experience.

You can see this feature of the human mind demonstrated in the most horrendous situations. When people are held captive by a sole individual and despite the fact that this person has abducted them, tortured and abused them, the victim slowly over time begins to develop feelings for the perpetrator. Despite suffering at the hands of this person, they become conditioned to their environment and begin to want to please the person who holds them against their will. This phenomenon has been studied at length by eminent psychologists and is known as 'Stockholm syndrome.'

To a certain degree, I believe you are suffering from a form of this syndrome; alcohol has abused you for so long that you now firmly think there is a benefit to you. You have fallen in love with a killer!

I say again, Alcohol tastes bad, your first interaction with it proved that point. When you first sneaked a drink of your father's neat whiskey, did it taste amazing? Or did it taste vile? Most people will say it tasted disgusting and they couldn't ever imagine getting hooked on something that tasted that bad. The taste of alcohol has not changed, so the only explanation for your current belief that it tastes good, is that you have changed. You have conditioned yourself to believe booze tastes good. Don't feel bad; you have had a significant helping hand from society and the advertising industry.

What you must understand from this point on is that what you previously believed about booze was a lie and nothing more. If I poured a glass of pure alcohol and asked you to dip your little finger in and taste it, I am sure you will agree it would taste horrible, indeed, if you drank that glass of liquid you would shortly be dead. Funny really because since birth you have been programmed to ignore this and instead believe that alcohol is natural and an everyday part of life that you must consume if you are to be considered by your peers as a fun and social member of the gang. This is a throwback to our primitive evolution, we are still pack animals to a certain extent, and this is another reason for our global addiction to this drug.

The second reason is best explained by a smarter man than I, a famous psychologist called Abraham Maslow. Maslow is known for establishing the theory of a hierarchy of needs, writing that human beings are motivated by unsatisfied needs and that specific lower needs need to be satisfied before higher needs can be.

Although there is a continuous cycle of human wars, murder, and deceit, he believed that violence is not what human nature is meant to be like. Violence and other evils occur when human needs are thwarted. In other words, people who are deprived of lower needs, such as safety, may defend themselves by violent means. He did not believe that humans are violent because they enjoy violence. Or that they lie, cheat, and steal because they enjoy doing it.

According to Maslow, there are general types of needs (physiological, safety, love, and esteem) and they must be satisfied before a person can act unselfishly. He called these needs "deficiency needs." As long as we are motivated to satisfy these cravings, we are moving towards growth, toward self-actualization.

Satisfying needs is healthy, and blocking gratification makes us sick and unhappy. In other words, we are all "needs junkies" with cravings that must be satisfied and should be satisfied. If we don't concentrate on doing this, we will become sick. 'Will-power' is an illusionary weapon created by the egoic mind. It's like your enemy giving you a plastic sword and saying 'here, use this to protect yourself if I ever attack you!' This is exactly why people have such a hard time trying to go cold turkey with their drinking. One morning you wake up and say, that's it I am never drinking again. By lunchtime, you have a psychological itch so intense you are almost screaming inside.

Will-power does not work because it forces your subconscious and conscious mind into civil war. The same reason why the moment you go on a diet you become hungrier than you thought possible.

Here is the secret to stopping drinking; you need to attach more pleasure to not drinking than there is to drinking. You have to remove the need by understanding the truth about booze. It is not a social pleasantry but rather an attractively packaged poison. A multi-billion dollar marketing campaign for the alcoholic drinks industry is working exceptionally hard to convince you otherwise, but you have to trust your gut on this one.

Let me put the point another way. I have two wonderful children who I love and adore more than life itself. Maybe you also have children yourself, and you can understand my love and need to protect my children from the harms of the world? Let me ask you a question: If you had some strong rat poison for dealing with a tricky vermin infestation, would you keep it in a chocolate box and put it within reach of your kids?

Alcohol is similar to an anti-personnel landmine. You step on it, and beyond a small clunk, all appears fine… until you try and step off it. Then and only then you discover what a mess you are really in.

Our desire to drink is what we call a proponent need; this is a 'need' that has a powerful influence over our actions. Everyone has proponent needs, but those 'needs' will vary among individuals. A teenager may need to feel that he/she is accepted by a group. A heroin addict will need to satisfy his/her cravings for heroin to function normally in society, and because of the strength of the need, they are unlikely to worry about acceptance by other people.

There is no difference between alcohol and heroin, or alcohol and nicotine. The only difference is drinking is socially acceptable. But ask yourself this, if it had not yet been invented and I brought it to market tomorrow, do you think I would get it even halfway through the rigorous testing process modern day food and beverages have to go through?

Around the world, there is a very popular television program called 'Dragon's Den,' where would-be entrepreneurs pitch their ideas to already successful venture capitalists seeking investment. Can you imagine taking your fabulous new drink additive called alcohol before the Dragons and asking them to invest?

Entrepreneur: "Hello Dragons… I am here to ask for $1,000,000,000 to launch my new drink supplement called alcohol. Would you like to try a glass?"

A small sample of the product is poured into shot glasses for each of the investors in turn; cautiously they take a sip…

Dragons: "My God that tastes disgusting!"

Entrepreneur: "Yes, it does initially, but we have tested it quite extensively and find that people do eventually become accustomed to the taste. Plus, we use sweet-tasting carrier beverages such as orange juice and cola to cover up the real taste. When they get used to it, the consumer will feel amazing! Parties will go with a bang, everything seems funnier, and there is a massive euphoric sense of well-being".

Dragons: "Sounds interesting, are there any downsides to this new drink?"

Entrepreneur: "Erm, well there is a slight risk of vomiting, sexually transmitted disease from unprotected sex, not to mention the violence and serious damage to careers, reputations, and relationships. You probably need to be aware that several millions of our potential customers will have to die in agony from organ failure. Apart from that, I think this product has great potential".

Dragons: "I am not investing in that, I am out!"

Am I going to ridiculous extremes to make my point here? Perhaps. But no more ridiculous than people around the western world claiming that the disgusting liquid they took a sneaky drink of when their parents weren't looking as a kid, has somehow turned into an exquisite and delicious beverage. The booze tastes just as vile as it ever did, but you have allowed this attractively packaged poison to fit you with some very impressed rose-tinted glasses!

Here's an experiment for you, wait until Friday evening and go check your friends out on Facebook. You will see status after status along these lines:

"Wine O-Clock... I think so."
"Friday night and I can hear the beer monster calling.'
"Friday night takeaway and a bottle of wine... it would be rude not to."
"Thank God it's the weekend, chilling out with a nice bottle of red."
"Enjoying a very large glass of wine... I love the weekends."
"Cheeky glass of wine on the go."

That last one particularly amuses me, that we could explain away what we are doing by adding a cute descriptive term before admitting the truth. You wouldn't hear this with any other drug, would you? Imagine if we talked about heroin in the same way.

"Friday night, a cheeky hit of heroin… it would be rude not to."

It's time to grow up and realize you have been scammed. Yes, you. The bright and worldly-wise individual who has a good job and a successful career. The very same person who achieved all that has been fooled by the oldest trick in the book.

You have become addicted to a drug, and this has created a recurring psychological itch that makes you want to scratch it at regular intervals. You have created a deficiency need, and according to Abraham Maslow, when the deficiency needs are met: Instantly other and higher needs emerge, and these, rather than physiological hunger, dominate the person. And when these, in turn, are satisfied, again new (and still higher) needs emerge, and so on. As one desire is satisfied, another pops up to take its place. It is this automatic behavior pattern that means we never really get the motivation to focus on what needs we are serving. The ego once again complicates the matter by insisting on more. More gratification, more consumption, more love, more power just more!

We are complicated beings, and our addiction to alcohol is just one cog in an intricate and needy machine. We are also addicted to love and significance. Which distracts our attention from the dependence we could actually do something about! Humans have a desire to belong to groups: clubs, work groups, religious groups, family, gangs, etc. We need to feel loved by others, not so much in a sexual way; I suppose another way of putting it would be to say that we need to feel significant. We need to be accepted by others. Performers appreciate applause. We need to be needed. Beer commercials, in addition to playing on sex, also often show how beer makes for camaraderie. When was the last time you saw a beer commercial with someone drinking beer alone?

But does alcohol really answer the social need within us; we like to get together and consume this drug but does it really create a sensation of love?

Ask yourself how you would feel about ordering a drink of alcohol in a room full of teetotalers. Perhaps group drinking creates a sensation of safety in numbers; it makes us feel like what we are doing is perfectly acceptable in the eyes of our peers. Plus we also get to witness people who are 'far more drunk' than us!

Alcohol is touted as the social drug, but in fact, it turns us into very anti-social individuals. We become loud and opinionated; in some cases, it makes us aggressive and violent. Even the 'happy drunks' slur and talk nothing but pure gibberish as they fall over even the most obvious obstacle. Uncontrolled laughter, loss of bladder control, vomiting in the streets and in the back of taxi cabs are just a few of the accepted norms of this most social of drugs.

When you stop drinking you will look at all this universally endorsed chaos and see it for what it really is – group insanity on a global level.

Would you do me a favor? Go back to the online store that you bought this book from and leave me a rating and review. It really is the most effective way to help me spread the word about this book. With your help, I can get more and more people out of the misery of alcohol addiction.

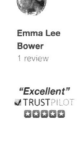

Emma Lee Bower
1 review

"Excellent"
 TRUSTPILOT
★★★★★

Published Sunday, March 11, 2018

Cannot recommend enough

Cannot recommend enough. After being a very heavy drinker from age 18, I'd tried numerous times to quit/cut down etc without any luck. Everything in my life was suffering because of alcohol. Then I found Craig Beck, within 24 hours of listening to Craig's book, alcohol lied to me, something changed, something just clicked for me. I had no want or desire to drink. I've been alcohol free for almost 3 years now, I know this wouldn't be possible without the help and support from Craig and his approach to alcohol. I cannot thank him enough. Turning 40 in a few weeks, my life now is uncomprehendingly better and richer than it ever was.

👍 Useful   2   🏳   ⋖

Chapter Five
When Enough Is Enough

"I am so incredibly motivated by this how to stop drinking course and the incredible Craig Beck! I am personally on Day 7 with no alcohol! I have been drinking alcohol for 30 years but only hit bad by the drug in the last ten years.

I have detoxed many times, tried counseling and medication, but nothing worked. I am now on Day 4 of this course and on fire as a result of all the things I have already seen and heard, the remarkable free book Craig very kindly provided was what started the process of me wanting to understand and learn more. I have been using his TFT and Hypnotherapy, and that is just amazing.

The private Facebook group is also such a help as you are sharing with others and even reading about their journeys, it makes you feel that you are not fighting this battle on your own.

This whole programme is just fantastic, I know, at last feel I can win this battle and be free from alcohol addiction forever. Thank you, Craig, for all you do, you are the best", Rob Brown

Let's talk more about motivation and the theory that we are all enslaved to two basic driving desires: the need to avoid pain and gain pleasure. Everything in your life, at one level or another, is based on how it plays to these two primary needs. An easy example to illustrate this point is to ask you to take a good look at your body now; it's unlikely there is nothing about it you don't like or think could be improved. After all, we are all our own worst critics, and whether it's the general shape or size of your body, or there are more specific areas you are not comfortable with, there will undoubtedly be some areas which you would like to improve.

So the big question is, why don't you do something about it?

Why don't overweight people who are painfully unhappy with their size and shape, correct the problem? Why don't people who get out of breath running up a flight of stairs get on an exercise program to improve their fitness? The answer is an internal belief that the application of the cure creates more pain than the eventual pleasure of succeeding in the goal.

Imagine an overweight individual who hates what they see when they look in the mirror, who gets depressed while clothes shopping because they struggle to find the designer clothes they want in their size. Can we agree that for that person slimming down and becoming that trim, fit and athletic person they dream of would be an amazing feeling?

It would bring enormous pleasure to anyone to be able to walk down the street and notice the admiring glances of passersby. To make any clothes look fantastic on their chiseled and defined torso. Surely such pleasure is worth the pain of dieting?

Judging by the escalating levels of chronic obesity, this does not appear to be the case.

In reality, human beings will do significantly more to avoid pain than they will do to gain pleasure. While it's undoubtedly true, having a super model body would bring great pleasure, the perceived journey to get there contains too much pain for most people to contemplate tolerating. So the result is that many people remain in a perpetual limbo period with most things in their life that they are not satisfied with. They are not happy with the amount of money they earn but prefer to hang in a mediocre position than suffer the initial pain of pushing through their comfort zone to become a more skilled, talented, and experienced or specialist employee. How many people remain in a dead-end job daydreaming of their own business that they would love to set up but NEVER do anything about it?

The same rule applies to alcohol; you know deep down inside you would be happier without poison flushing around in your system on a daily basis. You know you would have more money in your pocket, more time awake and less time crashed out in a drunken paralysis. You know how wonderful it would feel not to care if you have a drink today or not, so why don't you deal with it? Simple… because at the moment you associate more pain with removing alcohol than you associate pleasure with stopping drinking.

Because of the ever-changing needs and demands of the ego, this perception of what constitutes pleasure and pain is always shifting. The most likely reason that you purchased this book is that you encountered what I call a 'Threshold Moment'. Essentially, something happened that temporally altered the balance of the scales. This is an event so traumatic that it causes an unbearable amount of pain that sends you into a massive, determined period of change. Let me give you a few examples of threshold moments in relation to drinking before I give you my own:

Life is cruising along nicely in your usual blinkered and ironic state, where you are acutely aware that you are drinking far too much and probably doing serious damage to your health, career and loved ones, and yet you still reach for the bottle of wine every night as soon as you get home. Happy to ignore all the warning signs in favor of blind ignorance.
One night… You are sitting watching television, your ego sedated and comfortably numb by the glass of mild anesthetic grasped comfortably in your hand. Your five-year-old daughter comes up to you with a carefully and proudly drawn picture. It's a colorful drawing of you, her daddy. You are slumped in front of the television and in

your hand a bottle of wine! BANG, Suddenly it hits you like a tonne of bricks – this is how your child sees you. Through her pure, innocent eyes she sees you for the real addict that you are. Children have no binding compulsion to pull any punches or to spare your feelings; they just tell it how it is.

Children are blank canvasses, and they learn in their formative years solely by watching us, the grown-ups. This social pleasantry that has made us so utterly miserable is here now because it has been passed down through the generations as a curse wrapped up in shiny paper and labeled as a gift.

The reason this book gets updated annually is because every year thousands of more people use it to help them stop drinking. Many of them send me their stories, and the collective wisdom of all us ex-drinkers is worth more than the sum of their parts. This is a heartbreaking story I was emailed only this week from Linda (not her real name as she has asked to remain anonymous). Linda grew up with an alcoholic mother and later went on to have her struggle with drink until she joined my online club last year. If you are a parent and wonder how your drinking effects your children, Linda's story is difficult but vital for you to read:

Being brought up by my alcoholic mother has had a profound effect on my self-perception and my relationship with alcohol.

My childhood is a combination of good vs. bad but alcohol made the world around me evil. I was protected from nothing and exposed to all as a result of having no parents to shelter me. Alcohol made my childhood a living nightmare - it took away the amazing, loving, proud mother I had and gave me a woman that I was mortified to be associated with.

I remember seeing her tears, her worries over money, anxiety in social situations and what was the answer? Alcohol. That was her answer each time, no matter the devastation caused by the last binge. She was so embroiled in the vicious pattern that she couldn't be a mother. I grew up being able to do whatever I wanted, and there were no consequences for my actions as my mum was a drunk - she would turn up drunk to formal meetings with my principle but then forget the conversation, so I got away with everything. This all accumulated into a general lack of respect I had for anyone, even myself. I respected no one and listened to no one know - no one cared for me, after all, if your parents can't be there for you, who can? More than a lack of respect for others, I didn't respect or love myself, my mother never took time to emotionally invest in me which left me feeling unworthy of love, so I rebelled to get the attention I craved.

My mother's drinking took her away from me - she didn't see the child I was, she didn't acknowledge my achievements, and she didn't attend my sporting events - all because alcohol got in the way. I was dragged up in a world no child should have to witness.

When she wasn't drinking she was the mum I loved and the best mother on planet earth - she would apologize, have a movie day, buy us sweets, and tell us it would never happen again...but the pattern continued.

As a result of my upbringing, I went through a decade of my life unable to have a few drinks with my friends, I went from entering the bar to being paralytic as I had no control over my drinks. The way I have been brought up is you drink until you're unconscious - there is no middle ground. It took years to bring this behavior under control and even now alcohol scares me.

I lost my childhood and so much more because of my mother's addiction to alcohol, I would not wish any child to experience the life I did with my mum.

Regardless of the world she brought me up in, I still love her as I know somewhere inside she is still there...but alcohol has won this battle, I only hope it won't win the war too!

Linda, United Kingdom

Whether you have your own child's super honest portrait of you pinned to the refrigerator door or perhaps Linda's story made you question your behavior, these sorts of events can be considered for many to be what I call a threshold moment, an event so powerfully painful that it forces you to change. The 'pain versus pleasure' scales take a dramatic nudge in one direction, and your perception of what you are doing changes enough for you to take action. Normally people on the road to giving up Attractively Packaged Poison have several increasingly severe threshold moments along the way.

Let me tell you what my personal threshold moment was like:

I am wonderfully blessed, and it could be said I have been guilty in the past of not appreciating that fact. I could be accused of being fantastically blaze about my two wonderful children who are 11 and 7. Without a modicum of ego here, I can tell you they look at me like I am faultless. I could have lived up to that view much better without alcohol distracting me from the true beauty of the gift I had been consecrated with.

I can't tell you how many fun days out there could have been that I never permitted to happen, just because I could not see a way for the day to include alcohol. I don't want to torture myself by considering how many options I took purely because they included alcohol. Option A might have been more fun for my children and option C might have been more enjoyable for my wife, but in the past, if option B included alcohol then that was always the only choice I took, because I couldn't see how anything could be enjoyable without a drink.

At this point, I will remind you that while I am sharing this with you, I don't believe in beating yourself up with your mistakes of the past. The past is very important in as much as it brought you to where you are now, but it has absolutely no relevance on tomorrow. Just because I made bad decisions in the past, does not mean I am compelled to make them again now, tomorrow or at any point in the future. Every dawn brings an exciting new opportunity for you to get it right. Trust me, I know you are at the start of a tough journey, but the commitment you have made just investing your money in this book (money you could quite have easily spent on your favorite brand of booze) is a dramatic and profound statement of intent.

Remember, as Woody Allen says "80% of success is just turning up", so if you are here as the result of a painful threshold moment, don't let that pain subside enough for you to believe that purchasing this book is enough to make a difference. Absorb it over and over; use the subliminal tools available from my website to help you alter your programming around alcohol.

Every time you observe the ego and catch it in the act of attempting to take over control of your choices, you reduce its power by a fraction of one percent. If you consistently keep doing this over time, I know the future is bright. Every day is worth living, and if you don't believe me about that right here and now, just try missing one of them!

When I became a dad, I was determined to be closer to my children than my dad was with me. I would always be there; I would be the kind of dad that they could always turn to no matter what. I would be the father who took his son fishing and his daughter to see the latest pop concert. My children and my wife would be safe, secure and happy. They would never have to worry about bills, or whether we could afford this or that, I would work as hard as I needed just to make it happen. What I never considered in this grand plan was what would happen if you took me out of the equation. What if I was not around to provide for and protect my family?

In 1997 I had to consider that situation could be a very real and likely possibility.

At this point I was drinking in the region of two bottles of wine a day; of course, I was still lying to myself profusely. I figured that because I had no urge to drink first thing in the morning, and my drinking in no way affected my work, I could not be an alcoholic. If I am honest, I didn't and still don't like the word alcoholic. For me, it describes the guy lying in the gutter swilling cheap whiskey from a brown paper bag, not me. I could not possibly have a serious drink problem; I was a director of two companies and had just been appointed to the board of a children's charity. And yet, every evening as soon as I got home I opened the first bottle of wine and gulped the first half down like it was the first gasp of oxygen to a free diver returning from the depths of the deep blue. By the time I fell into bed the second bottle would be empty, perhaps I would throw away the last mouthful just so if my wife asked I would honestly say that I had not had a full two bottles of wine.

I consider myself to be a relatively intelligent person, and yet here I was throwing a mouthful of wine away so that I could face my spouse and lie with a free conscience. It's amazing how tunnel-visioned we become, how we ignore the unnatural behavior we should recognize as warning signs.

At the height of my problem, I couldn't even contemplate a night at the movies without a drink. Movie theatres are full of popcorn, sweets and super-sized buckets of fizzy drinks, but rarely can you take an alcoholic drink into the movie. This was a problem for me (although it seemed normal at the time), after a hard day at work I didn't think it was fair that I should be deprived of my evening drink by a movie. I would sometimes buy a quarter bottle of whiskey and pour it into one of those 'big gulp' colas and sip on it all the way through the film.

Once alcohol takes hold of you, it never let's go. The grip is always tightened, I can't remember when I started drinking in movie theatres, but it didn't phase me. Alcohol moves so slowly that you don't even notice how deep you are sinking. I hope you stay with me to the end of the book but regardless please never assume your situation will get better on its own. If you ignore the problem now, it can only get worse.

This was my threshold moment!

In January 1997 after a particularly heavy festive season, I started to get a dull ache in my right abdomen just under my right rib. I dismissed it as a hundred different minor, insignificant medical problems from a bit of food poisoning to an intolerance of wheat; I even considered paying £300 for a food allergy blood test. In summary, I considered everything apart from the obvious, that the 140 units of alcohol a week were destroying my insides the same way alcohol destroys all life at a cellular level.

In February 1997, the dull ache was preventing me getting to sleep and I started searching the internet for my symptoms. As I scanned the possible reasons for a pain in this region, I suddenly became genuinely scared. Website after website suggested liver cancer, liver failure, liver cirrhosis, pancreatic failure, alcohol-induced gall bladder disease. The lists went on and on, all horrific illnesses, all caused by alcohol, and many were irreversible. I made an appointment to see my doctor.

In my lifetime I have never had anything seriously wrong with me; I have only ever been to the doctor for a cold or simple chest infection. My past experiences with the medical profession mean I always confidently expect to be told that the condition will clear up on its own, or that a short dose of antibiotics would be all that is needed. This time was different.

I sat in the doctor's waiting room, shaking with fear. I walked in and explained my symptoms. He asked how much I was drinking, I lied and said I used to drink a lot, but now I have no more than a glass of wine a night. Can you believe that even at this point I still lied? Of course, you can – you still do it all the time! This is the power of this drug we freely hand out to children at celebrations as a 'treat' to make them feel grown up. In honest fear for my life, face to face with a medical professional who was there to help me, I still lied to protect my opportunity to drink. Despite the fact that it was slowly killing me, I couldn't cope with the possibility that it would be taken away from me, so I lied to the doctor.

If you are not from the United Kingdom, let me explain that doctors in England are normally seen at the cost of the state on the National Health Service. Doctor's surgeries are usually over-subscribed and getting an appointment is sometimes difficult. My allocated time with Dr White was five minutes, behind me there were another seven patents all waiting for their own five minutes. After 35 minutes of examinations and questions, I knew this was going to be a very different experience than I was used to at the doctors.

I still expected, even after all the fuss, for the doctor to nod reassuringly and say "well, I've checked you over and you seem fine, come back in a month if it doesn't improve". Dr. White had a concerned but kind face, he looked up from his notes over his small round glasses and said "there is a very real possibility there is something serious behind your pain. I don't have the facilities here to examine you to the level I need to, so I am having you sent to the gastroenterology department at the hospital".

Hospital! Surely not! That is where sick people go; the health service is overstretched as it is, surely they wouldn't waste a valuable bed on someone young and healthy like me? As I walked home, neither cured nor reassured, this was the point when I realized this was not a figment of my imagination. I had possibly seriously damaged my body by selfishly drinking my attractively packaged poison.

I sat at home and watched my children play, and it felt like my heart had been ripped out. Knowing how much I love my family, how could I do that to them? How could I leave my children with out a daddy? How could I be so selfish that I would make my children go through the pain of watching their dad's funeral? How could I be so pathetic that I would risk making my wife a single parent, with two devastated children to look after and no income? I am not ashamed to tell you my world was ripped apart that evening, and I cried myself to sleep in a world of self-pity, regret, and guilt.

This was my ultimate threshold moment; it altered the balance of all things. For a brief time, the pain of continuing to drink was greater than the pain of living without my drug. I stopped drinking for eight weeks, and the pain subsided a little. The hospital performed dozens of blood tests and scans, and I was awaiting a liver biopsy because my enzymes were all over the place (a clear indication that my liver was in trauma). The problem with relying on a threshold event to cure your problem is, as soon as the pain generated by the threshold begins to fade, your determination to stick to your goals fades too, and you're back in the hands of good old-fashioned will-power. Let me tell you here, and now, will-power is no friend of yours or mine.

Will-power is a civil war, because it breaks a human need rule, it breaks the law of scarcity. I will explain in greater depth about this later in the course, but for the moment, if you want proof that you are fighting a losing battle trying to stop drinking with will-power, let me prove it to you.

The classic self-help process that relies on will-power is dieting. When you look in the mirror and decide you need to shed some weight, as soon as you start restricting the amount of food you are allowed, the body goes into shock. Suddenly the subconscious assumes there is a drastic shortage of food. This scenario is in direct conflict with your primary functional need 'to stay alive at all costs'.

The brain, thinking you are in the middle of a famine, starts applying pressure in the form of pain to get you to reverse the situation. Subconsciously you are in preservation mode; it is irrelevant that you want to lose weight or indeed that it may even be beneficial for you to drop a dress size or two. Your subconscious does not rationalize; it just completes tasks. This is why 95% of people who go on a calorie restrictive diet not only put the weight back on within five years, but have on average added an additional five pounds.

So the threshold pain faded, and I was left with nothing but will-power… I started drinking again, but this time I had a new system. Alcohol is a little creative poison and had come up with a brilliant new way for me to carry on flirting with her at a new, safe level. I bought a lockable drinks cabinet and loaded it with single measure bottles of whiskey, I gave the key to my wife and explained that I was only allowed one measure a night, and if I asked for more, she was to say no. It worked well for a whole week, well worth the £250 that the cabinet cost. The plan fell down when my wife went out with friends for an evening, and she took the key with her. I felt cheated because I had not even had a single drink, and she was breaking the rules; I was allowed one a day… how dare she do this to me!

I was like a petulant child, it didn't take me long to realize that the back of the cabinet was made of cheap plywood and was only tacked into place. A simple bit of leverage with a steak knife and the panel lifted up enough to squeeze a small bottle out. The new plan was dead from this point on!

Within three weeks the pain was back and stronger than ever, and more tests eventually revealed that if I didn't want to risk liver failure within two to three years, I had to stop drinking immediately. I stopped drinking… for three weeks, and started again. Even faced with a death sentence, I still couldn't see how giving up booze was a life worth living.

I can't order you to stop drinking, your wife or husband screaming at you won't stop you drinking, your children begging you, still won't make you see sense. Even YOU grasping the nettle and deciding to give up and resist temptation is futile. The only way you can live without this drug is to fundamentally change your opinion of it. You need to see it for what it really is: 'attractively packaged poison'. You have probably tried to give up or cut down in the past and failed, this is because at the end of the day you still want it, need it and desire it. You still believe that alcohol is in some way benefiting you.

I have heard every excuse going from people just like you and just like me:

- I can't sleep without a drink before bed
- I need it to relax
- I am boring without a drink
- Drinking gives me confidence
- It helps me relax after a hard day at work

These are all lies, and deep down inside you know they are. If you are currently using any of these statements, from now on see them as evidence that you are currently sitting inside a giant mousetrap resolutely believing you are perfectly safe.

The day you stop seeing alcohol as a benefit and seeing it for what it really is, you will start to become free. As you work with me during this book, you will slowly begin to become aware that alcohol no longer tastes as good as it used to. You will start noticing the unpleasant taste that you have previously learned to ignore (often people report a strange sensation of disappointment with their drink). The harshness of the poison will slowly become more and more dominant over the heaps of sugar and fruit the drinks companies use to disguise the drug hidden within. It may sound unbelievable to you at this point, but using my system, you will get to the point where you find the taste of alcoholic drinks unappealing, disappointing and often just plain disgusting (just like you did when you first took a sneaky sip of your father's beer when you were younger).

Published Sunday, March 11, 2018

Truly Amazing!!!

I'm very grateful to have found Craig Beck! A decade of problem drinking, 4 times in AA. I lost hope. When seeing alcohol for the poison it truly is, as well as removing the shame and stigma of "alcoholic" made the journey a bit easier. I still get cravings and have bad days, but now I have the book to listen to, the videos to watch, and the hypnosis recordings. Huge help! Thank you Craig Beck, I'm getting my life back!

"Excellent"

93

Chapter Six

The Psychology Of Alcohol Addiction

"He is so honest and truthful and blows apart every myth we ever believed in alcohol. I am so blessed to have found Craig's programme. So much of what he says resonates with me, and I'm finally beginning to understand. Craig speaks from the heart having had an alcohol problem himself in the past; it's not just some randomer who doesn't know what you are going through. I genuinely believe that I can kick this and never go back to it because of this programme. Thanks, Craig", Sue Barlow

In the interest of honesty, I will forewarn you of my intention to use a sneaky persuasion technique on you called a 'pre-supposition.' Salesmen use these types of questions to appear to be offering you a choice when in fact all the responses serve the same purpose. A good example of a pre-supposition that might have been used on you as a young child (perhaps unwittingly) by your parents would be "do you want to go to bed now or in ten minutes time?" The question appears to give you the luxury of a choice, but all outcomes result in the same thing – you in bed within ten minutes.

My sneaky question to you is; do you want to stop drinking completely or just cut down a bit and repeat this course every time you lose control again until you stop? Obviously I am trying to gently push you in the direction I know you should go, and despite telling you the option to cut down has repeated failure built into it, your ego still thinks it is in control and can handle anything. Be certain of this, your ego doesn't want you to stop drinking because it predicts that will result in pain/fear in the future.

I know many readers would prefer to cut down rather than stop, but the only logical solution is for you to step out of the mousetrap and never get back in. If you are dependent on alcohol and you don't want to stop, you have not quite grasped the problem. If a heroin addict came up to you and said "I have decided to only use drugs on a Tuesday and never any other day", how confident are you that if you bumped into him again in a years time that would be still the case. Alcoholism is a binary condition, it is either on or off, you can't be a little bit alcoholic in the same way you can't be a little bit pregnant!

You may need to read this book over and over before you get to this point and your decision is in harmony with my advice. Stopping completely really is the best option for you, but you must come to that decision on your own. You can't be convinced by me, your family or friends and nobody can order you to take this stance, it has to come deep from within you. If you don't currently feel like that if you are still at the point where you believe you can control the situation, or that you enjoy it too much to stop completely, don't panic or beat yourself up too much. You are not alone in this struggle. In my online community, you will find people who are in the same position as you. Nobody has ever developed a drinking problem and then woke up the next morning and cured it in a eureka moment of perfection.

Part of the journey to sobriety is experiencing the futility of trying to find a way to keep the bits you like while removing the consequences you don't want. It is like trying to bail out the Titanic with a bucket; for a while, you may believe you are making headway, but very soon you start to see that you can't possibly succeed. I tried dozens and dozens of different buckets before I realized that the good parts of drinking go hand in hand with the bad, and you can't have one without the other.

Here are just a few of the buckets I thought might bail out my sinking ship:

• I will only drink on the weekends.
• I will only drink socially and never at home.
• I will drink a glass of water for every glass of alcohol I drink.
• I will take three months off the drink each year.
• I will only drink beer and no wine or spirits.
• I will only drink wine and with food as part of a meal.

Add to that list of ridiculous theories the expensive prescription drugs I turned to. The first I tried was Disulfiram, which interferes with the way your liver processes alcohol and makes you violently ill if you drink. The problem with this drug is that it relies on your discipline to take it every morning (alcoholics are not renowned for their discipline). Initially, if I knew there was a big party or social occasion I was going to, I just wouldn't take it (and so begins the failure routine). Predictably I then loosened my rules further by only taking it Monday to Friday, allowing myself to drink at the weekends, I convinced myself that I deserved a treat at the weekends for being so good during the week.

The next stage of my defiance came when I resented the drug preventing me from drinking during the week, and I experimented with it and found that I could just about tolerate a small beer while taking it. Any more than that and the side effects would knock me flat on my back. One night I pushed it a little further and had a large beer and a glass of wine. Within twenty minutes my head was pounding, my face blushing bright red, while my heart felt like it was trying to beat its way out of my chest cavity. For a moment I honestly thought I might die, and the only solution was to lie in a dark room motionless for several hours until the effects subsided.

I tried other drugs, such as Acamprosate Calcium, which interfere with the release of dopamine, essentially taking all the pleasure out of drinking. Over time it renders your favorite tipple as pleasurable as a soft drink, and logically you only want to drink one of those when you are thirsty. Again, with this drug the will-power or discipline required to take a daily tablet that ruins the very thing you are addicted to is a significant challenge. Add to that some pretty horrendous side effects from dizzy spells, insomnia, dry mouth and worse, and you start to think that feeling this bad to stay off the drink is simply not worth it.

Whether it's crazy routines or pills, they are all simply evidence of the ego's delusion that it is in some way in control. All these methods use some form of will-power that can't possibly work because underneath the smoke screen you still believe that alcohol is a benefit that you are being deprived of.

Remember, there is no such thing as failure, things that go wrong are just events in the past, a period we are no longer concerned with. If you finish reading this book and go three weeks without a drink and then slip up, the natural temptation (and the ego's opinion) is to think that this book doesn't work, you are not strong enough, or you are destined to always be a problem drinker. Recognize this belief for what it is; the conscious mind trying to predict the future – a skill it simply doesn't have. If you fall off the wagon… big deal, dust yourself down and carry on. When you wake in the morning, what is the point of beating yourself up about that mistake you made the night before? The past no longer exists.

Presumably, you haven't woken up with a bottle in your hand having been drinking in your sleep somehow, so right there in that moment (where all of life is lived), you are not a drinker. Equally, now that we know that the future also doesn't exist and will never exist, the fact that you had a drink the night before has no bearing on whether you will have one later that day, tomorrow, the next day or ever again. Take each moment as it comes, every second that you decide you don't want to drink is a success.

The secret to stopping drinking is the same as the secret to getting anything else in life that you want, and this is to remain in the moment. Don't make predictions about what sort of person you will be in the future. I wouldn't ask you to predict what will happen tomorrow any more than I would ask you to perform open heart surgery on me, you simply don't have the skills to help me (of course, I am recklessly playing the numbers here, one day this book will land with an eminent heart surgeon, and he will be mortally offended by that statement). Your journey out of the mousetrap happens by being aware of our egoic mind; every time you find your mind wandering into the future or past, observe this happening from the point of view of an outsider. Disconnect yourself from the process; catch your ego at work.

For your conscious mind to have any power at all, it needs you to believe that you and it are the same thing. If you see if for what it is; a minor part of your mind at work then it loses all its influence over you. Every time you catch your mind starting to worry, predict or reflect on past events and deliberately pull yourself back into the present moment you reduce its power over you by a fraction of one percent.

For most people, the conscious mind seizes control of them tens of thousands of times a day, and so this process isn't a magic bullet cure. I can't promise if you do this ten times, twenty times or fifty times you will be cured, but then you didn't become alcohol dependent overnight, and no system out there can hope to restore the correct balance in a similar brief time period. Most other detox systems require a period of withdrawal, often called going 'cold turkey', which for an alcoholic is at best torturous, and in worst case scenarios can be fatal.

My method starts with your deep-seated desire to end this painful cycle and slowly deconstructs the obstacles preventing you from achieving your goal. Slowly, over time, as you keep resisting the attempted hijackings by your egoic mind you will feel a sense of peace begin to build. Once you get beyond the physical dependence on alcohol, your urge to drink is generated by the wants and needs of the ego, as this reduces so does your desire for alcohol.

A popular question at this point is "how long will it take?" I can't predict the future any more than you can, so won't even try to give you a specific prediction. For most people, once they understand that everything they previously believed about alcohol being a benefit was a big fat lie and can see that a chemical imbalance is causing pain for their ego to respond to, they simply stop. For a great many people that is directly after reading this book, others need a few weeks for the information to sink in, and others read the book several times before the penny drops.

Whether it takes a day or a year is irrelevant, you will find this simple process will not only remove your damaging patterns around alcohol but also all other negative habits too. Denying the ego will slowly repair everything from relationships to finances if you want to go into greater detail about how it works then I would suggest you read my books 'Swallow The Happy Pill' and "The God Enigma'.

Once your conscious mind begins to loosen its grip on your perception of reality, this system becomes easier and easier. The secret to success is to stick at this long enough to become aware of a shift in power. So for the next 21 days, I am going to ask you to commit to doing four things every day. This does not mean after 21 days you are no longer dependent on alcohol, or that you can stop and return to your old ways. I just know if you diligently follow the four steps I will reveal as we continue through this book, for that amount of time you will start to see something amazing happen in your life.

Ready to say 'enough is enough'? Visit www.StopDrinkingExpert.com right now and get started on getting the 'real you' back.

Chapter Seven
The Cost of Drinking

"I want to say to anyone out there with a drinking problem Craig's course is unusual, why? Because it works!! I have been scouring the internet for some time and identified with Craig immediately, there are so many sites, but none appealed to me.

The funny part is I identified with everything he said, which only means one thing, he has honestly really been through it himself and is not a chancer.

I have never been so confident and happy for a long time now, too long. This guy is a genius at what he does, and I'm truly indebted to him for saving my marriage, my business, and my life", Steven

When I stopped drinking, I sat down and worked out how much I had been spending on booze. It's no surprise to me now that I didn't conduct this exercise while I was still drinking. I simply didn't want to hear the financial cost of my habit. I didn't want to hear any negatives about booze (this is pure ostrich syndrome), the same technique that stopped me going to the doctor because I was afraid he would tell me to stop drinking.

Western society acts as though alcohol is nothing more than a social pleasantry to be enjoyed with friends, but in reality, it is a drug so powerful it can even prevent intelligent individuals from getting urgent medical help. Make no bones about it; this is a very dangerous and sinister drug – the ultimate wolf in sheep's clothing!

At the peak of my drinking, I was knocking back two bottles of wine a night, plus a bottle of whiskey over the weekend. At a rough guess that equates to a daily spend on alcohol of $23.00 per day. A weekly spend of $161.00 or $724.00 every month. Wow! No wonder I didn't want to see this figure while I was still drinking, that would have shocked and depressed me – BUT, it still wouldn't have stopped me drinking, and that is perhaps the scariest thought of all.

If I hadn't stopped drinking, it's entirely likely I would have continued consuming booze at that ungodly rate, or even increased it further to compensate for my growing tolerance to the effects of the drug. This means that over the next decade (if I had lived that long) I would have blown $86,940 on my addiction. Even this startling admission is only a half-truth because it doesn't allow for any of those ridiculously priced $400 bottles of 'art', Christmas, Birthdays or any other formal excuse to get excessively drunk.

I was spending nearly $9000 a year on drinking a poison while telling my children and family that we couldn't afford the expensive vacations or other little luxuries that we might have been able to have if I wasn't lying to them, and of course, to myself. Hopefully, as you are starting to see, alcohol misled me. It lied to me, and it continues to lie to you – the challenge I throw down to you now is 'what are you going to do about it?"

I encourage you to honestly do this exercise for yourself and calculate how much money you are spending on a common drug addiction. You will no doubt come up with an amount of money, which you can think of a hundred different and better things to spend it on. Sadly the financial cost is almost insignificant when compared to the other factors that need to be considered when you try to take stock of what alcohol has stolen from you.

Booze affects everyone differently, but for me, it made me sleepy. In a practical sense, what this meant for me is when I got home from work at let's say 6 pm; the first glass of wine was poured by 6.05pm. Less than an hour later the first bottle was gone. By 8 pm I had moved onto, and consumed about two thirds of the second bottle of wine (I would never drink the full second bottle because then I claim I had not drunk two full bottles of wine if anyone asked). At this point in the evening, after nearly two bottles of wine, I could hardly keep my eyes open. I would spend the next 30 minutes staring at the clock wishing it was later so I could go to bed at a decent time. It would be rare for me to make it to 9 pm, normally collapsing unconscious into bed between 8.30pm and 8.45pm.

I would sleep badly, waking several times to use the toilet and a few more times gasping for water to deal with the dehydration. My bloodshot eyes would blink open at 6 am, and I would head to work exhausted.

This was my life for longer than I care to admit, and while alcohol may not have the same outcome for you, there will almost certainly be another negative side effect to replace it. In my case, let's say a more reasonable bedtime for a 9 to 5 office worker is around 11 pm. This means that my drinking took me offline for an additional 17 hours per week. Over ten years I spent 9,100 hours knocked out, unconscious because of my drug addiction. That time I will never get back, how many opportunities and experiences can you fit into nearly 10,000 hours?

The mind boggles.

The situation is even bleaker because I am a father; it's not just my time I was throwing away. Allow me to expand on this point to ram home the gloomy message of what my drinking did:

If you are a parent, I apologize for what I am about to ask you to do next. If you are visual or kinesthetic character type, then this may be traumatic and painful for you to imagine, but please bear with me because I am doing this not to be cruel or give you nightmares, but rather to make a valuable point. Imagine for me; that tomorrow your child is abducted, and you never see them again. Immediately such a horrific suggestion may remind you of what happened to the McCann family while on vacation in sunny Portugal a few years ago.

On Thursday 3rd May 2007, Jerry and Kate McCann put their little daughter Madeline to bed for the last time. At some point before midnight, she was taken from her bed and has never been seen since.

If that happened to you and there was absolutely nothing you could do to prevent it happening, let me ask you, what price would you put on an hour spent with your daughter? If a few months later it were possible to buy the opportunity to see your child again and spend just one hour with them, what would you be prepared to pay?

Is it $1000, $10,000, $100,000 or is it priceless? Would you pay everything you had just to spend that one-hour with your child? I know for me the answer is the latter, and yet alcohol (the social drug) made me throw away over 9,000 hours that I could have spent with my lovely children Jordan and Aoife.

My children are the most precious things in my life, and yet a drug that people insist is just a bit of harmless fun, a beverage that they say is vital to the success of a party, a drink they demand must be consumed or you will be labeled boring and weird… Somehow this 'innocent' substance made me willingly give away 758 priceless days with my children.

I am going to take a break from writing at this point because I am so angry and feel so cheated that I don't think I can continue.

I will close this chapter by giving you one question to think about. What has alcohol stolen from you?

Is it your health, your time, your promotion, your money, your wife, your husband, your career? It may be one thing, or it might be many, but as sure as night follows day, make no mistake about it… you are the victim of a serious theft. Unless you wake up and realize that the bottle of booze you thought was your friend is your worst enemy, then you will be a victim tomorrow, the day after and every day until the truth dawns on you.

The average drinker who joins my online stop drinking club is spending around $3000 a year on alcohol! That might sound a lot, and the tendency of any drinker is to assume they are nowhere near that amount. But $3000 is less than ten bucks a day and so if you are one of those people who drink a bottle of wine a day plus a bit more at the weekend, then you are way over that figure. Let's keep the glass half full (excuse the pun), and we will stick with the average. Every person I have ever spoken to has agreed that they could find something important to do with 3000 dollars.

If I gave you that money today and told you to blow it, what would you do with it?

- Maybe take the kids to Disneyland?
- Put it towards a new car?
- A romantic vacation?
- Put it towards the college fund?
- A medical bill or procedure?
- Pay off a credit card?

Whether you would use it to make life bearable or to simply add pleasure for you and those you love. That money is there and waiting for you to do any one of those things. You don't have to ask your boss for a raise, work overtime or change job – it is already yours! To get it, all you have to do is step outside your current situation and see that alcohol is not your friend, helping you deal with a difficult life but rather your enemy, deliberately stealing all those wonderful things from you and your family.

My challenge to you is to put this book down and do the exercise that 95% of drinkers refuse even to consider. Sit down and honestly work out how much you spend on alcohol in a year. Make sure you include those lunchtime drinks with clients, weekend binges and the special occasions such as Christmas and birthdays. Those times when you treat yourself to much more expensive poison than usual. Come up with your golden number and then think about what you would do with that money if somebody gave it to you in a lump sum today.

Next take that image, whether it is the trip to Florida you have always wanted to take or clearing the debt that just won't leave you alone. Get on the Internet and find an image that represents that aspirational item. Print it out and stick it on the refrigerator or bathroom mirror. Somewhere where you will see it every day. If you ever take that image down without having completed the goal, you will know that alcohol still has a hold over you.

Chapter Eight
F.S.Q (Frequently Slurred Questions)

"Craig is The Man. So personal and can relate to every word he teaches. This program is worth its weight in Gold. I tried to work out how to stop drinking a million times, but there are so many tools in this program I genuinely think this it. The Evil Clown will stay trapped inside my head forever, and I won't give him the satisfaction of revealing himself ever again. Craig, you are amazing, I can't thank you enough", Donn Stout

Forgive the quirky play on words because this section of 'How To Stop Drinking Without Willpower' may serve a very valuable purpose in your mission to escape the cycle of alcohol addiction. Over the years I have had many questions emailed to me from problem drinkers (mostly look for reasons why it would be okay for them to carry on with their drug of choice).

No doubt some of the queries in this ever-expanding section of the book may have popped into your head at some point, so here goes:

Q1. I want to stop drinking but I work with a pretty tough bunch of guys, and if I didn't drink with them I wouldn't hear the end of it. Should I just cut down rather than stop drinking?

A1. I can empathize with your situation because we live in a bizarre world where heavy drinking has somehow become associated with being a 'real man.' Back when I was a drinker I had quite a reputation for being able to 'hold my drink.' As we now know this tolerance for alcohol should be seen as the first symptom of a serious problem with an addictive drug and not the positive trait that social males so often dictate that it is. I stopped drinking in the winter, November. In the past I would have postponed this attempt to January because you can't go through a Christmas season without drinking can you (yet another funny lie we have been force fed).

When I woke up and realized that it is the rest of the world that is wrong about booze and not me I just decided I didn't want to drink it anymore, so the month had no relevance to me.

However, as easy as I found it to no longer drink I still had to attend the traditional Christmas party with all my old drinking buddies.

The evening started in a local pub, and my friend Roy walked up to the bar and ordered himself a pint of strong imported beer, he turned to me and said 'same?'. I shook my head and instead asked for a diet coke. A few moments of time passed without further comment, and then it began:

"A coke, I am not ordering you a coke. Have a beer and man up", Roy exclaimed, absolutely disgusted at the very suggestion.

"It's ok Roy I am fine with a coke", I replied

"What's wrong with you man, have you turned gay or something", Roy came back.

Perhaps the most ridiculous statement I have ever heard!

I am not sure of the logic behind assuming a decision to no longer voluntarily ingest a toxic chemical must be the result of a change in sexuality but sadly it's a statement thrown at heterosexual men who regain control of alcohol all over the world. Drinking vast quantities of alcohol does not prove you are a tough, red-blooded 'mans man'! It proves you are addicted to a common drug!

These sorts of macho put-downs are ridiculous and laughable but how do you deal with them?

You tough it out! Eventually, your friends will get used to the new healthier you. The problem as we have already discussed is it's your new high standards highlighting the other person's low standards that causes them pain and their ego will not tolerate it. Obviously, the best way for them to remove that nagging pain is also to stop drinking but because the ego hates all form of loss, it can't accept that prospect and would much rather you started drinking again as a substitute solution.

These days Roy doesn't even need to ask me what I want to drink; he just goes up to the bar orders himself a pint and a diet coke for me. He might mutter some comical insult as he hands it to me but he has accepted the situation and so will your friends – do not bend to their attempts to persuade you back into the mousetrap.

Q2. I have heard that Milk Thistle protects the liver, can I continue drinking if I take it?

A2. Milk thistle (Silybum marianum) has been used for 2,000 years as an herbal remedy for a variety of ailments, particularly liver, kidney, and gall bladder problems. Several scientific studies suggest that substances in milk thistle (especially a flavonoid called silymarin) protect the liver from toxins, including certain drugs such as acetaminophen (Tylenol), which can cause liver damage in high doses. Silymarin has antioxidant and anti-inflammatory properties, and it may help the liver repair itself by growing new cells.

Although some animal studies demonstrate that milk thistle can be helpful in protecting the liver, results in human studies are mixed.

Milk thistle is often suggested as a treatment for alcoholic hepatitis and alcoholic cirrhosis. But scientific studies show inconclusive results. Most studies show milk thistle improves liver function and increases survival in people with cirrhosis or chronic hepatitis. But problems in the design of the studies (such as small numbers of participants and differences in dosing and duration of milk thistle therapy) make it hard to draw any real conclusions.

Whether milk thistle helps or not is a gamble you can choose to take if you want. If you are seriously considering continuing to drink and supplementing your diet with milk thistle, then I would suggest you have missed the point of this book. Such an act would imply that there is a benefit to continuing to drink alcohol and this is quite frankly insane!

Alcohol is attractively packaged poison backed by a devious and misleading multi-billion dollar marketing campaign. The solution you are suggesting is likely to be as effective as the smokers who believed that if they didn't inhale deeply, they wouldn't be at such a high risk of developing lung cancer. Any thoughts on ways that you can carry on drinking are just more evidence that you need to get this poison out of your system once and for all.

Q3. How do I avoid drinking at Christmas, Thanksgiving and other social occasions?

A3. Well, let me start by asking you how you manage to avoid injecting heroin at Christmas time?

That might sound like a silly question, but in reality, there are only two differences between alcohol and heroin. Firstly it is just a case of social acceptability, everyone drinks at Christmas, and so we make the false assumption that it is therefore harmless. Just because everyone is doing it does not make it a safe activity, you only have to go back a few decades, and the same twisted logic was applied to smoking. The social proof of smoking did not prevent millions of people from dying in agony from lung cancer.

Alcohol is attractively packaged poison whether one person drinks it or a whole nation consumes it.
The second difference between heroin and booze is to do with the kick. All addictive substances will punish you if you try to stop your interaction with them, this is known as 'the kick.' Class A street drugs such as heroin trap their users so successfully because the punishment from stopping using is so severe that it takes great determination and endurance to suffer the kick.
The pain of a heroin kick is beyond anything you can imagine, and addicts must endure days of this agony

with the knowledge that the pain would vanish in less than a second if they just took another hit of the drug.

Having said that if you believe that alcohol has the power to make you feel good, then you should try heroin. Wow, heroin can create the feeling of pure ecstasy, a sensation of pleasure beyond our dreams or so I am told.

So here is the big question… why don't you long for heroin at Christmas and Thanksgiving, it is far superior to alcohol afterall?

The explanation that we keep coming back to is; you do not see any benefit to taking heroin. You would not see it as an enhancement to your life – your thinking about this drug is perfectly logical and as it should be about such a dangerous poison. The problem is your thinking about (alcohol) is twisted.

If you are thinking about how you can survive your birthday party without a drink, this is just a clear marker that your thinking is still distorted. You should be thinking about how good it is going to feel to have your first birthday in years that won't result in a horrific hangover.

As far as Christmas is concerned the alcohol has only been added in relatively recent times because it provides a convenient excuse to consume more of our favorite drug. Whether you are religious or not consider whether booze figures anywhere in the traditional story of the birth of Christ? Of course, it doesn't, the three wise men did not turn up with a crate of beer, a bottle of vodka and some coffee liqueur. These are the trappings of a society trapped in their relationship with an addictive drug.

Look to the east with other similar festivals such as the Hindu celebration of light Diwali. Five days of festivities, full of fun, laughter, dancing, and merriment… any yet not a single drop of alcohol will cross anyone's lips!

If people tell you that you can't have a good Christmas without a drink, what they are saying to you is: "I can't cope without alcohol, not even in an environment that is fun and pleasant already".

Q4. Do you believe the spiritual aspect of AA is wrong?

A4. Absolutely not actually, I think it probably makes a significant impact on those that truly embrace it. The problem is a lot of people will start running as soon as they get a hint of religion and or spirituality. It smacks too much of a cult and allows the ego to instantly come up with a thousand reasons why the process won't work.

While I am not religious, you will quickly be able to gather from a Google search of my other books that I am very spiritual-minded. I face most challenges in my life with a specific spiritual technique called Ho'oponopono. I choose not to refer to it in the book until now for the very reasons stated above.

Ho'oponopono is the ancient Hawaiian spiritual process of acceptance, forgiveness, and gratitude. Rosario Montenegro offers one of the most concise stories of how Dr. Hew Len brought this amazing tradition into modern popular culture around the world.

More than thirty years ago, in Hawaii, at the Hawaii State Hospital, there was a special ward, a clinic for the mentally ill criminals. People who had committed extremely serious crimes were assigned there either because they had a very deep mental disorder or because they needed to be checked to see if they were sane enough to stand trial. They had committed murder, rape, kidnapping or other such crimes. According to a nurse that worked there in those years, the place was so bleak that not even the paint could stick to the walls; everything was decaying, terrifying, repulsive. No day would pass without a patient-inmate attacking another inmate or a member of the staff.

The people working there were so frightened that they would walk close to the walls if they saw an inmate coming their way in a corridor, even though they were all shackled, all the time. The inmates would never be brought outside to get fresh air because of their relentlessly threatening attitude. The scarcity of staff was a chronic occurrence. Nurses, wardens, and employees would prefer to be on sick-leave most of the time in order not to confront such a depressive and dangerous environment.

One day, a newly appointed clinical psychologist, a Dr. Stanley Hew Len, arrived at the ward. The nurses rolled their eyes, bracing themselves for one more guy that was going to bug them with new theories and proposals to fix the horrid situation, who would walk away as soon as things became unpleasant, around a month later, usually. However, this new doctor wouldn't do anything like that. He didn't seem to be doing anything in particular, except just coming in and always being cheerful and smiling, in a very natural, relaxed way. He wasn't even particularly early in arriving every morning. From time to time he would ask for the files of the inmates.

He never tried to see them personally, though. Apparently, he just sat in an office, looked at their files, and to members of the staff who showed an interest he would tell them about a weird thing called Ho'oponopono. Little by little things started to change in the hospital. One day somebody would try again to paint those walls, and they actually stayed painted, making the environment more palatable. The gardens started being taken care of, some tennis courts were repaired, and some prisoners that up until then would never be allowed to go outside started playing tennis with the staff. Other prisoners would be allowed out of their shackles, or would receive less heavy pharmacological drugs. More and more obtained permission to go outside, unshackled, without causing trouble to the hospital's employees.

In the end, the atmosphere changed so much that the staff was not on sick leave anymore. More people than were needed would now go to work there. Prisoners gradually started to be released. Dr. Hew Len worked there close to four years. In the end, there remained only a couple of inmates that were eventually relocated elsewhere, and the clinic for the mentally insane criminals had to close.

Simply put, Ho'oponopono is based on the knowledge that anything that happens to you or that you perceive, the entire world where you live is your own creation and thus, it is entirely your responsibility.

- Is your boss a tyrant? It's your responsibility.
- Are your children not good students? It's your responsibility.
- There are wars, and you feel bad because you are a good person, a pacifist? The war is your responsibility.
- You see that children around the world are hungry and malnourished if not starving? Their want is your responsibility.

No exceptions. Literally, the world is your world, it is your creation. As Dr. Hew Len points out: didn't you notice that whenever you experience a problem, you are there?

It's your responsibility, doesn't mean it's your fault, it means that you are responsible for healing yourself in order to heal whatever or whoever it is that appears to you as a problem.

It might sound crazy, or just plain metaphorical, that the world is your creation. But if you look carefully, you will realize that whatever you call the world and perceive as the world is your world, it is the projection of your own mind.

If you go to a party you can see how in the same place, with the same light, the same people, the same food, drink, music and atmosphere, some will enjoy themselves while others will be bored, some will be overenthusiastic and some depressed, some will be talkative and others will be silent.

The "out there" for every one of them seems the same, but if one were to connect their brains to machines, immediately it would show how different areas of the brain would come alive, how different perceptions there are from one person to the next. So even if they apparently share it, the "out there" is not the same for them, let alone their inner world, their emotions.

How can you use Ho'oponopono to help with giving up drinking?

Three steps: by recognizing that whatever comes to you is your creation, the outcome of bad memories

122

buried in your mind; by regretting whatever errors of body, speech and mind caused those bad memories, and by requesting divine Intelligence within yourself to release those memories, to set you free. Then, of course, you say thank you.

There are seminars where they teach you many tricks to help this process, but according to Joe Vitale, Dr. Hew Len himself uses the simplest of the formulas from Ho'oponopono. Whenever a matter arises –and they arise incessantly– addressing the Divine within you, you only have to say: I'm sorry, Please forgive me, Thank You, I Love you.

If you want to discover more about the origins and evidence of Ho'oponopono, look out for a book by Joe Vitale called Zero Limits. Joe goes into great detail about how this amazing principle that has been passed down the ages literally creates miracles.

Q5. I have stopped drinking and I am really happy about that but I dream about alcohol every night. Is this normal and how do I stop it?

A5. Yes it is completely normal and sometimes the dreams will be so vivid and detailed that you will wake up completely convinced that you had been drinking during the night.

I remember when I first stopped I had a dream where I was knocking back shot after shot of neat whiskey. The dream was so lucid that when I awoke I emptied every garbage bin in the house to make sure there were no empty bottles there. I think I dreamed about drinking for a week solid before they started to slow down. For the first few months of my sobriety, I would have a drinking dream about once a week and now it is down to about once a year. Although they still take me by surprise when they happen and I wake thinking 'what the heck was that all about'!

As to why this strange phenomenon happens is up for debate. Personally I believe that it is due to a combination of reasons. Firstly your dreams are a way for your brain to filter and sort the information you have absorbed during the day. Your brain files away important information and discards the junk. When you first stop drinking you are acutely aware of not having a drink in your hand and you are constantly reminded of situations where before you would have consumed alcohol. As alcohol is still playing an active role in your life, albeit by its absence it is still considered worthy of processing by your subconscious mind. As you stop noticing the nonappearance of alcohol in your day-to-day life it will appear less in your dreams accordingly.

The second reason for alcohol dreams is down to a change in brain chemistry. Back when I was drinking I would rarely manage to get past 8pm, I would drink a bottle or two of wine and would stumble upstairs to crash into bed – often even before my children's bedtime. I would blink my bloodshot eyes open ten hours later but I would feel like I had had only about an hours sleep. This is because alcohol is a mild anesthetic and despite what the doctor tells you before an operation anesthesia does not cause sleep but rather a reversible coma.

When you are under general anesthetic it is not possible to dream because brain activity is slowed to virtually nothing. Dreams are complex and creative actions of the brain and the chemical is preventing anything but the basic functions to support life.

None of the self-repair and cell regeneration happens during this time, as the brain cannot coordinate the process. When you awake from a drunken 'sleep' perhaps less than half the night you weren't sleeping at all but rather in an anesthetic induced coma.
When you have been drinking heavily for a long period of time the brain and body get used to having this chemical permanently pumping around the system. Stopping drinking is like driving around for year with the parking brake on the entire time and then suddenly taking if off. When you stop drinking suddenly the brain has to get used to operating without the brakes on.

The absence of alcohol in the brain is an unusual and significant event that the subconscious has to get its head around (excuse the pun). So it is understandable that this focus would leak into our dreams. Don't worry; perhaps the single biggest reason human beings are at the top of the food chain is our ability to adapt. Within weeks these dreams will slow and fade away.

Got a question? Ask me live in my online stop drinking club at www.StopDrinkingExpert.com

Chapter Nine
The Next Step

"I have found Craig Beck's how to stop drinking method to be refreshing and successful for me. This may sound cliché, but as an individual who has a drinking problem/functional alcoholic whatever moniker you choose, his words are a helpful/guiding light on a cloudy horizon.

I would strongly recommend the Craig's program to anyone who has or suspects they have a problem with alcohol", Craig Kantack

Alcohol addiction is similar to getting stuck in quicksand. In both cases, we make an inaccurate assessment of the risk and the situation. We tend to only address our drinking when we have already started sinking up to our waist. You will notice that in areas where quicksand is a possibility they do not put up the warning signs in the middle of the danger. They put them right out there on the perimeter, long before you get near the danger zone.

The same is true of alcohol. When you first take a sip of booze and discover to your shock that it tastes vile. This should be an alarm bell that scares us off for life.

However, we take a look around and notice that everyone else is drinking and apparently enjoying their alcoholic drink. So we persevere despite all the evidence suggesting that drinking horrible tasting poison for fun is at best ill-advised.

So, we learn how to tolerate alcohol and to mix our metaphors, we keep walking towards the center of the quicksand. Then when we realize we are sinking we start to panic and struggle to control our drinking. We use willpower to force ourselves to drink less of the thing we want most in the world. The truth is using willpower to escape an alcohol problem is as misguided a plan as kicking and struggling are as an effective way to get out of quicksand.

The harsh reality is the more you panic the deeper you sink. The more you try to force yourself to go back to being a 'normal or social' drinker of attractively packaged poison the more you experience failure. Constantly failing to achieve your goal leads to low mood and stress. This then accelerates the problem because us drinkers have a solution for times when we are a bit down in the dumps... we drink!

It's very hard to get out of quicksand on your own. Really what you need is someone to come along, spot you are in trouble and reach out a hand to help you out. That is exactly what I do for people like you!

This book is a powerful first step because not least, you have taken action on a problem that the vast majority of people refuse to deal with. However, if you are otherwise a successful individual with a lot to lose then refusing to take that helping hand is a gamble with significant consequences.

Consider what could happen to your career, income, reputation and loved ones if you don't deal with this problem. How would life look like in five years time if your drinking just kept getting worse?

Helping people escape the trap of alcoholism is my passion. If you ever attend one of my quit drinking events you will see just how much I throw into this. I live it and I breathe it. This is why over the years I have gained the reputation as the World's #1 Quit Drinking Mentor. Every year I work with a handful of people on a one to one basis. I effectively become your sponsor. We talk (video) on a regular basis and I make sure you nail this problem once and for all.

This is the most powerful and effective alcohol cessation solution anywhere today.

- Personal mentor calls with Craig Beck
- Custom scripted & recorded hypnosis
- Complete step by step video course
- Secret Facebook group
- Inner circle upgrade
- Non-judgmental community

- Free entry into any live event
- 75 hours video & audio coaching
- 90 days intensive support
- Lifetime access & support

If you are interested in my Executive Quit Drinking Program visit the website and arrange a free consultation with me.

Recommended links
- https://www.CraigBeck.com
- https://www.StopDrinkingExpert.com

Follow Craig Beck on Social Media
- Facebook: https://www.facebook.com/craigbeckbooks
- Twitter: http://twitter.com/CraigBeck

You Don't Have to Do It Alone…
Join the online coaching club that has helped over
50,000 people just like you to get back in control of
their drinking.

Download the total control alcohol course as soon as you join

I have been where you are...

Why **you should believe me** on this?... I am not a doctor telling you to drink less, I know it's not that easy!

My program works so well because I have been in the same alcohol-trap as you and escaped... Two bottles of wine a night and even more at the weekends was normal for me.

I know you don't want to stand up and call yourself an alcoholic. Actually I don't believe you are, **as soon as you get started** I will tell you exactly why this is the case.

Why not <u>decide now</u> and start to feel the benefits within 24 hours of joining

7 Life changing aspects to joining today

1. Significantly more effective than cold turkey or willpower methods.

2. 100% private & confidential solution – completely online process.

3. Protects your career – no need to take time off work to attend therapy.

4. Personal support from best selling author and ex-drinker Craig Beck.

5. No prescription drugs – no medication with problematic side effects.

6. Save thousands – the average Stop Drinking Expert member saves over $3000 per year.

7. Repair relationships – become a better parent, partner and friend.

100% private solution

I understand you don't want to risk your career or have any sign of this problem on your medical records. With my online stop drinking cure, you can deal with this in 100% privacy.

Another of the things you are going to love about my control alcohol system is you will be able to cut down or even how to quit drinking completely.

When you get started today and join the thousands of other who are back in control of their drinking.

www.stopdrinkingexpert.com

Lightning Source UK Ltd.
Milton Keynes UK
UKHW032330040219
336741UK00002B/496/P